Fundamentals of MARC 21 Bibliographical Format

Dr. Subarna K.Das
Department of Library and Information Science
Jadavpur University, Kolkata

Ess Ess Publications
4837/24, Ansari Road, Darya Ganj,
New Delhi-110002
Tel. : 23260807, 41563444
Fax : 011-41563334
E-mail: info@essessreference.com
www.essessreference.com

Ess Ess Publications
4837/24, Ansari Road,
Darya Ganj,
New Delhi-110 002.

Tel.: 23260807, 41563444
Fax: 41563334
E-mail: info@essessreference.com
www.essessreference.com

Rs.1125/-

First Published - 2009

ISBN: 978-81-7000-559-9

Published By Ess Ess Publications and printed at Salasar Imaging Systems

Cover Design by Patch Creative Unit

PRINTED IN INDIA

Dedicated To

My Beloved Mother

Late Kamala Bala Das

Contents

Preface

This book entitled "**Fundamentals of MARC 21: Bibliographic Format**" is an attempt to provide basics of MARC 21 Bibliographic Format to the working professionals in the field of library and information Science. The efforts have been made to cover each and every aspects of MARC 21 Bibliographic Format. The first chapter is Introduction,which gives an overview on MARC 21 and its impact on practical cataloguing of printed as well as electronic and non-book materials. The next chapter deals with MARC 21 field-wise examples which helps the LIS professionals as to how to prepare entry easily for each field. These examples are actually prepared by Library of Congress, which is the foundation of MARC 21 bibliographic Format. I have modified some fields due to the complex nature of the documents.This chapter will provide a clear idea about each field of MARC 21.Chapter third deals with the preparation of model MARC 21 bibliographic format along with practical examples. This format is prepared for periodicals. The next chapter is concerned with bibliographic format of composite book.This Chapter is very helpful for academic library professionals as well as LIS students of Indian universities, since in academic library system, most of the books are of composite nature.The fifth chapter presents Committee Reports on MARC21 Bibliographical Format. I have discussed five committee reports in the present book. Chapter six deals with uniform titles whereas chapter seven is concerned with multi-volume books.The next chapter brings forth the anonymous book while the concluding chapter dwells on pseudonymous book.There is no comprehensive book available giving complete knowledge of MARC 21 bibliographic format and its utility in library and information science field. The author hopes this work will also prove useful to the students those arte pursuing their courses in library and information science besides the working professionals. The teaching community those who are teaching MARC 21 may also find this book is useful in equal way.Effort has been made to provide precise, concise and upto date information on different topics. Users of this book are requested to extend their valuable suggestions for betterment and making this book more useful in future.

Author

Acknowledgements

In completing this critical task, the works of various authors have been consulted and their Ideas suiting the layout of the book have been incorporated. As far as the personal assistance is concerned, the author is thankful to Sangita Kaul, Network Manager DELNET, NewDelhi for NACLIN 2003(Tutorial), Smt. Uma Majumder, Assistant Library and Information Officer, National Library, Kolkata (MARC 21 format used for National Library), Moutasi Basak, Library officer, Tata Consultancy Service, Kolkata, Miss Ambika Dhar, Library Trainee , National Institute of Orthopdedically Handicapped.The author is also thankful to Dr. K.P. Majumder, Professor, Dept. of Library and Information Science, Jadavpur University, Dr. S.K, Chatterjee,Reader, Dept. of Library and Information Science, Jadavpur University,Dr. Chaitali Dutta, Reader, Dept. of Library and Information Science, Jadavpur University, Dr. Udayan Bhattacharya, Reader, Dept. of Library and Information Science, Jadavpur University, Dr. P.K. Panigrahi, Professor, Dept. of Library and Information Science, University of Kolkata, Prof. Subal Ch. Biswas, Dept. of Library and Information Science,University of Burdwan, Prof. R.S.R. Varalakshmi, Dept. of Library and Information Science, Andhra University,Prof. S. B.Ghosh, IGNOU,Prof. Pravakar Rath, Dept. of Library and Information Science Mizoram University, Prof. S.P. Singh,Dept. of Library and Information Science, University of Delhi, Prof. S.L. Sangam, Dept. of Library and Information

Science,Karnatak University, Prof. Lalita Astha, Dept. of Library and Information Science, Bangalore University, Dr. HarisChandra, Librarian IIT, Chennai, Mr. Manoj Kumar, INFLIBNET, Dr. Manoj Kumar Sinha, Asstt. Librarian, Assam University,Dr. Parthasarathi Mukherjee,Dept. of Library and Information Science, University of Burdwan,Mr.Kishore Satpathy, Librarian, IIM, Indore,Dr. Mohan Raj Pradhan Healthnet, Nepal,Mr.Binod Behari Das, Chief Librarian, Jadavpur University, Prof. Juran Krishna Sarkhel, Dept. of Library and Information Science, University of Kalyani, Dr, J.N.Satpathy, President, IASLIC, Prof. Arjun Dasgupta,Dept. of Library and Information Science,University of Calcutta, Prof. Biplab Chakraborty, Dept. of Library and Information Science,University of Calcutta, Dr.Nausad Ali, Reader, Dept. of Library and Information Science, Aligarh Muslim University, Prof. H.N. Prasad, Dept. of Library and Information Science, Benaras Hindu University, Dr Gautam Maity,Dept. of Library and Information Science, Vidyasagar University for giving inspiration and their valuable suggestions.The author is very thankful to Mr. Sumit Sethi, the owner of Ess Ess Publications, New Delhi for his keen interest in bringing out this work quickly and neatly.

Subarna K. Das

1

Introduction

MARC is the acronym of machine readable Cataloguing. It was first designed by the library of Congress. "Machine-readable" means that one particular type of machine, a computer, can read and interpret the date in the cataloging record. The following pages will explain why this is important and how it is made possible.Cataloging record: "Cataloging record" means a bibliographic record, or the information traditionally shown on a catalog card. The record includes (not necessarily in this order): 1) a description 1) a description of the item, 2) main entry and added entries, 3) subject headings, and 4) the classification or call number. (MARC records often contain much additional information).

MARC-I

Marc-I pilot project began in April 1966. In which 16 libraries participated. By the year 1968 the library of congress had distributed over 50 thousand English language monograph records. The purpose of MARC I was in automation of cataloguing, indexing, searching and Retrieval functions.

MARC-II

The Marc-I format on entirely on the structure of the library of congress catalog cards and covered monographs only, encourage by the success of MARC-I. Marc Format is a set of standardized data structure use to describe bibliographic material, which facilitated co-operative cataloguing and data exchange in bibliographic information systems. It operates as a protocol for continuously updated and revised in response to in new and developing terminology. Several countries have interpreted MARC and brought out their own versions such as US MARC, Canadian MARC etc.)

The proliferation of MARC formats gave rise to a move for convergence of MARC formats.UNIMARC (the Universal MARC Format) was developed and published in 1977. It conforms to ISO 2709 standard as also ISBD standard. The latest edition of UNIMARC Manual (2nd edition) was published in 1994. There is already a move to further revise the manual. The primary purpose of UNIMARC is to facilitate the international exchange of bibliographic data in machine-readable from between national bibliographic agencies. UNIMARC may also be used as a model for the development of new machine-readable bibliographic format. Since 1977 several national libraries have undertaken projects to convert from an existing national format to UNIMARC or have adopted UNIMARC for their national format needs. It covers monographs, serials, and cartographic materials, music, sound recording, graphics, projected and video material with provisional fields for computer files.The permanent UNIMARC Committee (PUC), under the auspices of the IFLA Universal Bibliographic Central and International MARC CUBCIM) Programme, supervises the format. A harmonized version of CAN/MARC and US/MARC has also since come out, which is known as MARC 21. 1987 the library of congress issued the first edition of the document 'MARC 21 specifications for records structure character sets and exchange media' to aid libraries and other organizations that create for acquire Marc 21 records. Subsequent editions were published in 1990, 1994 and 2000.MARC I pilot project began in April 1966 in which sixteen libraries participated. By the year 1968, the library of congress had distributed over fifty thousand English language monographs records. The purpose of MARC I was the automation of cataloguing, indexing, searching and retrieval functions. The participating libraries made better use of MARC tapes distributed by L.C. in a variety of ways in producing catalogue cards, books form of union catalogues, specialized lists of materials under subjects, lists for acquisition on purpose and the like.

The MARC I format was entirely on the structure of the L.C. catalogue cards and covered monographs only. Encouraged by the success of MARC I, staff of the L.C. started redesigning the procedures and programmers to cover material in other forms, and developed character set to include all the major Roman alphabet language as well as romanized forms. Meanwhile the British National Bibliography (BNB) showed interest in the UKMARC pilot project. Similarly interest was also shown by many foreign libraries to design a standard communication format suitable for interchanging bibliographic data not only from one source organization, the L.C., to many participating libraries, but also for exchanging information on cooperative basis among libraries at the international level. The US, the UK, and other countries wanted to machine-readable catalogue format that would be a common one for international exchange of cataloguing and bibliographic data. Such as interchangeable record format was designed and was called MARC II.

It was a one format structure on the machine-readable medium capable of containing bibliographic data of all forms of library materials, such as books, monographs, serials, physical representation on the machine – readable medium ; the content designators, such as tags, indicators. And sub-field codes used to identify the data elements; and the content or the data itself such as author, title and bibliographic descriptions are the three components of the L.C. MARC format.MARC II officially began in March 1968. Distribution began for all English language material providing a weekly magnetic tape of zonal 1000 records. Thereafter, other documentation began to be issued, including formats for other materials over the period 1970-73. In 1972 film records were distributed, by 1973 records for serials, maps and French books, by 1975 German, Spanish and Portuguese materials.MARC II (or MARC) is a subscription service. By subscribing to this service a library can acquire, in machine readable form cataloguing data for American and other foreign publications as described above. In fact, the library of congress catalogues and documents, i.e. books and non-book materials, records the data on magnetic tape and supplies copies of the tapes to various interested libraries. The libraries which get the copy of magnetic tape, can then produce printed catalogues of their collection entries on cards and various kinds of bibliographic (author or subject, etc) by using a computer. Most libraries obtain access to MARC data through products and services developed by publisher's computer system developers, time sharing services and other intermediaries. At present a growing number of vendors supply the MARC database in CD-ROM disks or digital optical video discs accompanied by software which supports the retrieval of specific cataloguing records and the printing of card sets.

Types of MARC Formats

1.CCF (Common Communication format) : CCF was developed by UNESCO/UNISIST and is being implemented primarily in developing countries where MARC does not have such a strong. This format has been used for exporting the data from METADATA format or other MARC format.

2. USMARC : the USMARC formats are (American) standard for the representation and communication of bibliographic and related information in machine-readable form. Formats are defined for five types of data: bibliographic holdings, authority, classification and community information.

3. UKMARC : the UKMARC format is the standard

developed, managed and promoted by the British Library and applied by the library in its bibliographic products and services and by many UK libraries in their bibliographic processing operations (UKMARC Web page, British library National bibliographic Service (NBS), 1999).There are many similarities in the structure and content of USMARC and UKMARC. However the differences are significant and sufficient to make high quality conversion between two formats complies. In addition, the use of variants in the UK and the minor differences in the US (USMARC and OCLC MARC) means high conversion between particular datasets need apply additional algorithms. UKMARC and USMARC are set to converge the impact of this is not yet clear.

1. CANMARC : CANMARC – the Canadian MARC communication formats serve as the common standard for the exchange of machine readable authority, bibliographic, classification and holding data in Canada.

Note: CANMARC and USMARC have been harmonized into MARC 21. However, continued support for these record types has been provided to ensure backward compatibility. USMARC should be used when the user specifically desires MARC 21.

2.UNIMARC : the primary purpose of UNIMARC is to facilitate the international exchange of bibliographic data in machine – readable form between national bibliographic agencies. UNIMARC may also be used as a model for the development of new-machine-readable bibliographic formats (IFLA Universal Bibliographic Control and International MARC Core Programme (UBCIM) 1994).UNIMARC conforms to the ISO 2709 standard and to ISBD standards. UNIMARC: (The Universal MARC Format) was developed and published in 1977. UNIMARC was first developed as an exchange format and offers several options for description, so that records created on the basis of different cataloguing rules can all be included. UNIMARC deals with all the necessary bibliographic data.

3.DUBLIN CORE METADATA: - the Dublin Core is a proposed minimal set of data elements for describing network - accessible materials. It was initially proposed at a workshop held in March 1995 at Dublin, Ohio. Workshop participants included librarians and archivists, researchers, computer and information scientists, software developers, publishers, and members of internet engineering Task Force working groups. Their intent was to suggest a minimal set of data elements that might be provided by the creators or publishers of digital objects and included in, or linked to, the objects themselves.Metadata included with digital materials has significant potential as a source of information about those materials. Such metadata can be used as the basis for designing an information storage and retrieval system alternative, the meta data can be imperfect into existing data structures (such as USMARC bibliographic records) and used by existing information storage and retrieval systems.

The MARC 21 formats are standards for the representation and communication of bibliographic and related information in machine-readable form. A MARC record involves three elements: the record structure, the content designation and data content of the record. The structure of MARC record is an implementation of national and international standards e.g. information interchange format (ANSI Z39.2) and format for information exchange (ISO 2709). Content designation the code and conventions established to identify explicitly and characterize further the data elements within a record and to support the manipulation of those data is defined in the MARC 21 formats. The content of most data elements is defined by standards outside the formats, e.g., Anglo – American Cataloguing Rules, library of Congress Subject Headings, and National library of Medicine classification. The content of other data elements, e.g. coded data is defined in the MARC 21 formats. A MARC 21 format is a set of codes and content designators defined for encoding machine – readable records formats are defined for five types of data. Bibliographic, holdings, authority, classification and community information.

FORMAT ORGANIZATION OF THE RECORDS

The format of a MARC record owes a lot to the state of computer technology at that time. MARC is a binary format designed for writing to magnetic tape.The basic layout of a MARC record is to first have a 24 byte leader, then a variable number of directory entries and then a variable number of variable size fields. The field are sometime split into variable control field and variable data fields. The layout of whole MARC record is thus: **The Leader, the Directory and the Variable fields.**

Leader consists of data elements that content coded values and are identified by relative character position. It is the first 24 characters of the record. Each position has assigned meaning, but much of the information in the leader I for computer use. Data element is a leader defines parameters for processing the record.

Directory contains the tag starting location and length of each field within record. The leader is a block of data called a directory. Directory entries for variable control fields appear first in ascending tag order.

Variable Contro! Field-The 008 field is referred to as Fixed Length Data Elements, or Fixed Field Codes. Its 40 characters contain important information, but in an abbreviated form. Entries for variable data fields followed, arrange in ascending order of the first character of the tag.

These **standards** used for creating Marc Records

Cataloguing Code	-	**AACRII R**
Subject Heading	-	**LCSH**
Classification Schedule	-	**DDC**

MARC: Why Necessary?

Computer needs aid for interpreting the information found

on a cataloguing record. The information from a catalogue card cannot simply be typed into a computer to produce an automated catalogue. The computer needs a means of interpreting the information found on a cataloguing card. The MARC record contains a guide to the data, or title 'signposts," before each piece of bibliographic.

The place provided for each of these pieces of bibliographic information (author, title, call number, etc.) is called a "field". The records in simpler computer files sometimes have a fixed number of fields, and each field contains a fixed number of characters.

Advantages :

MARC tapes are to be used for various purposes, such as follows:

* A centrally prepared catalogue can be distributed to the receiving libraries in a machine readable form.
* In spite of increasing acquisitions in catalogue can be kept up to date without employing additional staff.
* In production cost of card catalogue on the computer (MARC System) is lesser than that of purchasing the library of congress catalogue cards.
* The MARC tapes can be used for producing conventional card catalogue by the subscribing library.
* The MARC tapes can be used for computerized SDI service.
* It automatically performed resource sharing functions.

Limitations

The following are a few limitations of MARC System:

* The Marc record for any little is almost similar to the conventional bibliographic records; as such it inherits all its limitations.
* The Marc format will be limited least for the next few years,

to the English language books because the MARC character sets as seriously limited in respect of special character.

* Expenditure on account of machine time by the participating library will go on increasing in view of the weekly shipment of about 12 hundred records or about 62000 records annually requiring 15000 fields of Magnetic tape.

MARC records are no longer created only by the library of a congress. But also many other agencies and are available proof bibliographic utilities and from commercial activities.

What Does MARC mean?

A MARC record is a Machine-Readable Cataloguing record.Machine Readable Cataloguing format is a set of data structures used to describe bibliographic materials that facilitate cooperative cataloguing and data exchange in bibliographic information system.

What is UNIMARC?

The primary purpose of UNIMARC is to facilitate the international exchange of bibliographic data in machine readable form between national bibliographic agencies. UNIMARC may also be used as a model for the development of new machine readable bibliographic format (IFLA universal Bibliographic control and International MARC Core Programme [UBCIM], 1994).UNIMARC conforms to the ISO 2709 standard and ISBD standard. Union: the Universal MARC Format was developed and published in 1977.

Machine-readable : "Machine-readable" means that one particular type of machine, a computer, can read and interpret the data in the cataloguing record. The following pages will explain why this is important and how it is made possible.

Cataloguing record : "Cataloguing record" means a bibliographic record, or the information traditionally shown on a catalogue card. The record includes (not necessarily in this order): 1) a description of the item, 2) main entry and added entries, 3) subject headings, and 4) the classification or call number. (MARC records often contain much additional information).

1) Description: Librarians follow the rules in *Anglo-American Cataloguing Rules*, 2nd ed., 2002 revision to compose the bibliographic description of a library item. This "description" is shown in the paragraph sections of a card. It includes the title, statement of responsibility, edition, material specific details, publication information, physical description, series, notes, and standard numbers.

2) Main entry and added entries: AACR2 also contains rules for determining "access points" to the record (usually referred to as the "main entry" and "other added entries"), and the form these access points should take. Access points are the retrieval points in the library catalogue where patrons should be able to look up the item.

In other words, the rules in AACR2 are used to answer questions such as: For this book, should there be entries in the catalogue for more than one author or more than one title? Should the title of the series be noted? How should the author's name be written? Is this a "title main entry" item (no author)?

3) Subject headings (subject added entries): The librarian uses the *Sears List of Subject Headings* (Sears), the *Library of Congress Subject Headings* (LCSH), or some other list of standard subject headings to select the subjects under which the item will be listed. Use of an approved list is important for consistency, to ensure that all items on a particular subject are found under the same heading and therefore in the same place in the catalogue.For instance, the subject heading list indicates that all books about cats should be assigned the subject CATS. Using this authorized heading eliminates the possibility of listing some books under CATS and others under FELINES. Even if a book is called *All About Felines*, the subject heading will be typed

CATS. That way, all books on that subject will be listed in one place in the catalogue for the patron to find. The patron does not have to imagine all the possible synonyms for the word he is looking for.

4) Call number: The librarian uses a Dewey Decimal or Library of Congress classification schedule to select the call number for an item. The purpose of the call number is to place items on the same subject together on the same shelf in the library. Most items are sub-arranged alphabetically by author. The second part of the call number usually represents the author's name, facilitating this sub arrangement.

Why Is a MARC Record Necessary?

The information from a catalogue card can not simply be typed into a computer to produce an automated catalogue. The computer needs a means of interpreting the information found on a cataloguing record. The MARC record contains a guide to its data, or little "signposts," before each piece of bibliographic information.The place provided for each of these pieces of bibliographic information (author, title, call number, etc.) is called a "field." The records in simpler computer files sometimes have a fixed number of fields, and each field contains a fixed number of characters.

Why one standard? You could devise your own method of organizing the bibliographic information, but you would be isolating your library, limiting its options, and creating much more work for yourself. Using the MARC standard prevents duplication of work and allows libraries to better share bibliographic resources. Choosing to use MARC .enables libraries to acquire cataloguing data that is predictable and reliable. If a library were to develop a "home-grown" system that did not use MARC records, it would not be taking advantage of an industry-wide standard whose primary purpose is to foster communication of information.Using the MARC standard also enables libraries to make use of commercially available library automation systems to manage library operations. Many systems are available for libraries of all sizes and are designed to work with the MARC format. Systems are maintained and improved by the vendor so that libraries can benefit from the latest advances in computer technology. The MARC standard also allows libraries to replace one system with another with the assurance that their data will still be compatible.

MARC 21 : The Library of Congress serves as the official depository of United States publications and is a primary source of cataloguing records for US and international publications. When the Library of Congress began to use computers in the 1960s, it devised the LC MARC format, a system of using brief numbers, letters, and symbols within the cataloguing record itself to mark different types of information. The original LC MARC format evolved into MARC 21 and has become the standard used by most library computer programs. The MARC 21 bibliographic format, as well as all official MARC 21 documentation, is maintained by the Library of Congress. It is published as *MARC 21 Format for Bibliographic Data*.A comparison of the same record with textual information and with MARC tags illustrates the compactness of the MARC 21 format. It's a matter of storage space. Her is a box charts below. The MARC 21 format uses "260" "$a" "$b" and "$c" to mark the field that holds imprint data instead of storing the words "publication area," "place of publication," "name of publisher," and "date of publication" in each record. This convention makes more efficient use of computer storage space.

Same record with MARC tags:

"SIGNPOSTS"			DATA
100	1#	$a	Arnosky, Jim.
245	10	$a	Raccoons and ripe corn /
		$c	Jim Arnosky.
250	##	$a	1st ed.

260	##	$a	New York :
		$b	Lothrop, Lee & Shepard Books,
		$c	c1987.
300	##	$a	25 p. :
		$b	col. ill. ;
		$c	26 cm.
520	##	$a	Hungry raccoons feast at night in a field of ripe corn.
650	#1	$a	Raccoons.
900	##	$a	599.74 ARN
901	##	$a	8009
903	##	$a	$15.00

MARC TERMS AND THEIR DEFINITIONS

1. FIELDS are marked by TAGS

A field: Each bibliographic record is divided logically into fields. There is a field for the author, a field for title information, and so on. These fields are subdivided into one or more "subfields." As previously noted, the textual names of the fields are too lengthy to be reproduced within each MARC record. Instead they are represented by 3-digit tags.

A tag: Each field is associated with a 3-digit number called a "tag." A tag identifies the field—the kind of data—that follows. Even though a printout or screen display may show the tag immediately followed by indicators (making it appear to be a 4- or 5-digit number), the tag is always the first 3 digits.

The tags used most frequently are:

010 tag	marks the **Library of Congress Control Number** (LCCN)
020 tag	marks the **International Standard Book Number** (ISBN)

100 tag	marks a **personal name main entry** (author)
245 tag	marks the **title information** (which includes the title, other title information, and the statement of responsibility)
250 tag	marks the **edition**
260 tag	marks the **publication information**
300 tag	marks the **physical description** (often referred to as the "collation" when describing books)
440 tag	marks the **series statement/added entry**
520 tag	marks the **annotation or summary note**
650 tag	marks a **topical subject heading**
700 tag	marks a **personal name added entry** (joint author, editor, or illustrator)

2. Some fields are further defined by INDICATORS

Indicators : Two character positions follow each tag (with the exception of Fields 001 through 009). One or both of these character positions may be used for indicators. In some fields, only the first or second position is used; in some fields, both are used; and in some fields, like the 020 and 300 fields, neither is used. When an indicator position is not used, that indicator is referred to as "undefined" and the position is left blank. It is the convention to represent a blank, or undefined, indicator position by the character "#".

Each indicator value is a number from 0 to 9. (Although the rules say it can be a letter, letters are uncommon.) Even though two indicators together may look like a 2-digit number, they really are two single-digit numbers. The allowable indicator values and their meanings are spelled out in the MARC 21 documentation. In the example which follows, the first 3 digits are the tag (245 defines this as a title field) and the next 2 digits (a 1 and a 4) are indicator values. The 1 is the first indicator; 4 is the second indicator.

245 14 $a The emperor's new clothes /
$c adapted from Hans Christian Andersen and illustrated by Janet Stevens.

3. SUBFIELDS are marked by SUBFIELD CODES and DELIMITERS

A. subfield : Most fields contain several related pieces of data. Each type of data within the field is called a **subfield**, and each subfield is preceded by a **subfield code.** Fields 001 through 009 have no subfields.

For example, the field for a book's physical description (defined by the tag 300) includes a subfield for the extent (number of pages), a subfield for other physical details (illustration information), and a subfield for dimensions (centimetres):

300 ## $a 675 p. : $b ill. ; $c 24 cm.

Content Designators

Is an inclusive term used to refer to tags, indicators, and subfield codes.

The three kinds of content designators—tags, indicators, and subfield codes – are the keys to the MARC 21 notation system. In his book, *MARC for Library Use* (2nd ed. (Boston: G.K. Hall & Co., 1989), p. 5), Walt Crawford calls the MARC system a "shorthand notation" system. The three types of content designators are the shorthand symbols that label and explain the bibliographic record.

B. Access points: Access points (a main entry, subject added entries, and other added entries) are an important part of the bibliographic record. These are the headings for which separate cards were created for the traditional card catalogue, and which a patron or librarian can search in an online catalogue. Most of the access points are in:

1XX fields (main entries)

4XX fields (series statements)

6XX fields (subject headings)

7XX fields (added entries other than subject or series)

8XX fields (series added entries)

"Authority control" means following a recognized or established form. Usually, a cataloguer chooses subject and name headings from a list of approved headings.

C. Parallel content: The fields requiring authority control are also the fields that use parallel tag construction. In general, in the 1XX, 4XX, 6XX, 7XX and 8XX fields, a personal name will have the last two digits 00. Therefore, for a main entry (1XX) that is a personal name (X00), the correct tag is 100. For a subject heading (6XX) that is a personal name, the tag is 600, and so on. This parallel content can be summarized as follows:

X00 Personal names

X10 Corporate names

X11 Meeting names

X30 Uniform titles

X40 Bibliographic titles

X50 Topical terms

X51 Geographic names

Preceding the main bibliographic record parts – which are known to all librarians because of their presence on catalogue cards – the MARC record contains some less familiar information. Automated cataloguing systems usually provide default data or prompts to help a cataloguer input this information.

A. Leader : The leader is the first 24 characters of the record. Each position has an assigned meaning, but much of the information in the leader is for computer use. MARC record creation and editing programs usually provide a window or prompts to assist the cataloguer in filling in any leader data elements that require input.

Directory : MARC records are called "tagged" records. Before it becomes a tagged record, a MARC record (in what is called the MARC communications format), looks very different — like one long run-on sentence. In the communications format, the fields are not preceded by tags. However, immediately following the leader is a block of data called a directory. This directory tells what tags are in the record and where they are placed (by a count of the characters to the position where each field begins). The directory is constructed (by computer) from the bibliographic record, based on the cataloguing information, and, if any of the cataloguing information is altered, can be reconstructed in the same way. The five MARC 21 communication formats, MARC 21 Format for Bibliographic Data, MARC 21 Format for Authority Data, MARC 21 Format for Holdings Data, MARC 21 Format for Classification Data, and MARC 21 Format for Community Information, are widely used standards for the representation and exchange of bibliographic, authority, holdings, classification, and community information data in machine-readable form. A MARC record is composed of three elements: the record structure, the content designation, and the data content of the record. The **record structure** is an implementation of the international standard *Format for Information Exchange* (ISO 2709) and its American counterpart, *Bibliographic Information Interchange* (ANSI/NISO Z39.2). The **content designation**—the codes and conventions established explicitly to identify and further characterize the data elements within a record and to support the manipulation of that data—is defined by each of the MARC formats. The **content** of the data elements that comprise a MARC record is usually defined by standards outside the formats. Examples are the *International Standard Bibliographic Description* (ISBD), *Anglo-American Cataloguing Rules, Library of Congress Subject Headings* (LCSH), or other cataloging rules, subject thesauri, and classification schedules used by the organization that creates a record. The content of certain coded data elements is defined in the MARC formats (e.g., the Leader, field 007, field 008). The *MARC 21 Format for Bibliographic Data: Including Guidelines for Content Designation* defines the codes and conventions (tags, indicators, subfield codes, and coded values that identify the data elements in MARC bibliographic records. This document is intended for the use of personnel involved in the creation and maintenance of bibliographic records, as well as those involved in the design and maintenance of systems for communication and processing of bibliographic records.

SCOPE OF THE BIBLIOGRAPHIC FORMAT

MARC 21 Format for Bibliographic Data is designed to be a carrier for bibliographic information about printed and manuscript textual materials, computer files, maps, music, continuing resources, visual materials, and mixed materials. Bibliographic data commonly includes titles, names, subjects, notes, publication data, and information about the physical description of an item. The bibliographic format contains data elements for the following types of material:

Books (BK) - used for printed, electronic, manuscript, and microform textual material that is monographic in nature.

Continuing resources (CR) - used for printed, electronic, manuscript, and microform textual material that is issued in parts with a recurring pattern of publication (e.g., periodicals, newspapers, yearbooks). (**NOTE:** Prior to 2002, Continuing resources (CR) were referred to as Serials (SE)).

Computer files (CF) - used for computer software, numeric data, computer-oriented multimedia, online systems or services. Other classes of electronic resources are coded for their most significant aspect. Material may be monographic or serial in nature.

Maps (MP) - used for all types of printed, electronic, manuscript, and microform cartographic materials, including atlases, sheet maps, and globes. Material may be monographic or serial in nature.

Music (MU) - used for printed, electronic, manuscript, and microform music, as well as musical sound recordings, and non-musical sound recordings. Material may be monographic or serial in nature.

* **Visual materials (VM)** - used for projected media, non-projected media, two-dimensional graphics, three-dimensional artifacts or naturally occurring objects, and kits. Material may be monographic or serial in nature.
* **Mixed materials (MX)** - used primarily for archival and manuscript collections of a mixture of forms of material. Material may be monographic or serial in nature. (**NOTE:** Prior to 1994, Mixed materials (MX) were referred to as Archival and manuscript material (AM)).

Kinds of Bibliographic Records

MARC bibliographic records are distinguished from all other types of MARC records by specific codes in Leader/06 (Type of record) which identifies the following bibliographic record types.

Language material	Nonmusical sound recording
Manuscript language material	Musical sound recording
Computer file	Projected medium
Cartographic material	Two-dimensional nonprojectable graphic
Manuscript cartographic material	Three-dimensional artifact or natural objects
Notated music	Kit
Manuscript music	Mixed material

Microforms, whether original or reproductions, are not identified as a special type of record. The microform aspect is secondary to the type of material to which the original item belongs (e.g., book). The same is true for **Computer Files** in that the computer file aspect is secondary; however, certain categories of electronic resources are coded as **Computer Files**.

COMPONENTS OF BIBLIOGRAPHIC RECORDS

Description of Record Parts

A MARC bibliographic record consists of three main components: the **Leader,** the **Directory,** and the **variable fields.** The following information summarizes the structure of a separate MARC record.

* **Leader** - Data elements that primarily provide information for the processing of the record. The data elements contain numbers or coded values and are identified by relative character position. The Leader is fixed in length at 24 character positions and is the first field of a MARC record.
* **Directory** - A series of entries that contain the tag, length, and starting location of each variable field within a record. Each entry is 12 character positions in length. Directory entries for variable control fields appear first, sequenced by the field tag in increasing numerical order. Entries for variable data fields follow, arranged in ascending order according to the first character of the tag. The stored sequence of the variable data fields in a record does not necessarily correspond to the order of the corresponding Directory entries. Duplicate tags are distinguished only by the location of the respective fields within the record. The Directory ends with a field terminator character (ASCII 1E hex).
* **Variable fields** - The data in a MARC bibliographic record is organized into **variable fields,** each identified by a three-character numeric tag that is stored in the Directory entry for the field. Each field ends with a field terminator character. The last variable field in a record ends with both a field terminator and a record terminator (ASCII 1D hex). There are two types of **variable fields.**
* **Variable control fields** - The 00X fields. These fields are identified by a field tag in the Directory but they contain

neither indicator positions nor subfield codes. The variable control fields are structurally different from the variable data fields. They may contain either a single data element or a series of fixed-length data elements identified by relative character position.

* **Variable data fields** - The remaining variable fields defined in the format. In addition to being identified by a field tag in the Directory, variable data fields contain two **indicator positions** stored at the beginning of each field and a two-character **subfield code** preceding each data element within the field.
* The **variable data fields** are grouped into blocks according to the first character of the **tag**, which with some exceptions identifies the function of the data within the record. The type of information in the field is identified by the remainder of the tag.

0XX Control information, identification and classification numbers, etc.

1XX Main entries

2XX Titles and title paragraph (title, edition, imprint)

3XX Physical description, etc.

4XX Series statements

5XX Notes

6XX Subject access fields

7XX Added entries other than subject or series; linking fields

8XX Series added entries, holdings, etc.

9XX Reserved for local implementation

Within the 1XX, 4XX, 6XX, 7XX and 8XX blocks, certain parallels of content designation are usually preserved. The following meanings, with some exceptions, are given to the final two characters of the tag of fields:

X00	Personal names	X40	Bibliographic titles
X10	Corporate names	X50	Topical terms
X11	Meeting names	X51	Geographic names
X30	Uniform titles		

Within variable data fields, the following two kinds of content designation are used:

* **Indicator positions** - The first two character positions in the variable data fields that contain values which interpret or supplement the data found in the field. Indicator values are interpreted independently, that is, meaning is not ascribed to the two indicators taken together. Indicator values may be a lowercase alphabetic or a numeric character. A blank (ASCII SPACE), represented in this document as a #, is used in an undefined indicator position. In a defined indicator position, a blank may be assigned a meaning, or may mean *no information provided.*
* **Subfield codes** - Two characters that distinguish the data elements within a field which require separate manipulation. A subfield code consists of a delimiter (ASCII 1F hex), represented in this document as a $, followed by a data element identifier. Data element identifiers may be a lowercase alphabetic or a numeric character. Subfield codes are defined independently for each field; however, parallel meanings are preserved whenever possible (e.g., in the 100, 400, and 600 Personal Name fields). Subfield codes are defined for purposes of identification, not arrangement. The order of subfields is generally specified by standards for the data content, such as cataloging rules.

Multiscript Bibliographic Records

A MARC bibliographic record may contain *data* in multiple scripts. One script may be considered the primary script of the *data content* of the record, even though other scripts are also used for data content..

Field and Subfield Repeatability

Theoretically, all fields and subfields may be repeated. The nature of the data, however, often precludes repetition. For example, a bibliographic record may contain only one 1XX main entry field; a field 100 may contain only one subfield $a (Personal name) but may contain more than one subfield $c (Titles and other words associated with a name). The repeatability or non-repeatability of each field and subfield is specified in the format.

Field Linking

Fields in the record may be specially linked using a generally-applicable field linking technique. The technique relies upon the syntax of data in subfield $8 (Field link and sequence number) to identify the linked fields.

Fill Character and Related Values

A fill character (ASCII 7C hex), represented in this document as a vertical bar (|), may be used in bibliographic records in fields 006, 007, and 008, and subfield $7 of field 533 (Reproduction note) and the linking entry fields (760-787). A fill character may not be used in the leader, or in tags, indicators, or subfield codes. The use of the fill character in records contributed to a national database may also be dependent upon the national level requirements specified for each data element. The presence of a fill character in a bibliographic record indicates that the format specifies a code to be used but the creator of the record has decided not to attempt to supply a code.

Code u (Unknown or unspecified) when it is defined indicates that the creator of the record attempted to supply a code but was unable to determine what the appropriate code should be.

Code n (Not applicable) is defined in many coded positions to indicate that the characteristic defined by the position is not applicable to a specific type of item or kind of record.

Display Constants

A display constant is a term, phrase, spacing, or punctuation convention that may be system generated in order to make a visual presentation of data in a record more meaningful to a user. In the bibliographic format certain field tags (e.g., field 770, Supplement/Special Issue Entry), indicators (e.g. field 511 Indicator 1, Display constant controller), and subfield codes (e.g., the subject subdivision subfields $x, $y, and $z in a subject added entry), may be used to generate specific terms, phrases, and/or spacing or punctuation conventions for the display of a record. The use of display constants is determined by each organization or system. Examples of display constants are provided under *Input Conventions* in the field descriptions.

Record Content Responsibility

The *MARC 21 Format for Bibliographic Data* serves as a vehicle for bibliographic data of all types from any organization. In general, the responsibility for the data content, content designation, and transcription of bibliographic information within a record may be determined by examination of the field indicated in the **responsible parties** section below. The data content of certain data elements, however, is restricted when the element is an **agency-assigned** or a **controlled-list** data element.

Responsible Parties

In *unmodified records*, the organization identified as the original cataloging source in 008/39 and/or 040 $a is responsible for the content of the record. The organization identified as the transcribing agency in field 040 $c is responsible for the content designation and transcription of the data.

In *modified records*, the organizations identified in 040 $a and $d (Modifying agency) are collectively responsible for the content of the record. Organizations identified as transcribing or modifying agencies in field 040 $c and $d are collectively responsible for the content designation and transcription of the data.

Agency-assigned Data Elements

An agency-assigned data element is one whose content is determined by a designated agency and is the responsibility of that agency, e.g., field 222 (Key Title) which is the responsibility of an ISSN Center. While it is usually input by the designated agency, it may be transcribed by another organization.

Controlled-list Data Elements

Certain data elements contain data from controlled lists maintained by designated agencies, e.g., the *MARC Code List for Geographic Areas* in field 043 (Geographic Area Code). These elements are indicated at the field or subfield level in MARC 21 and only values from the designated lists may be used. If a change or addition is desirable for a list, the maintenance agency for the list should be consulted.

Record Level Requirements

User groups may have full level and minimal level record requirements to promote consistency across cataloging agencies. These should be widely publicized for all possible interchange partners to be aware.

ORGANIZATION OF THIS DOCUMENT

Main Parts

MARC 21 Format for Bibliographic Data consists of a Summary Statement of Content Designators followed by a detailed presentation of each content designator. Following the descriptions of the Leader and the Directory, the detailed presentations for each variable field are arranged in field tag order.

General Information Sections

To avoid repetition, general information sections are provided for groups of fields with similar characteristics. These general information sections provide instructions for the content designators that are common to each field in the group. The description for each of the fields refers back to the general information section for that group and to any related general information section. For example, the X00 Personal Name–General Information section is provided for personal name headings. This general information section provides instructions for the content designators that are common to each type of personal heading whether it is used in a 100 main entry field, a 600 subject access field, an 700 added entry field, or a 800 series added entry field. The description for each of the individual fields (i.e., 100, 600, 700, 800) refers back to the X00 general information section.

Components of the Detailed Descriptions

A detailed description may consist of six parts: content designator listing; character position or field definition and scope; guidelines for applying content designators, with examples; input conventions; and content designator history.

The **content designator listing** area presents

* the name of the content designator
* the repeatability/nonrepeatability code (R or NR)

For the Leader and the variable control fields, the list gives the **name** of the character position and any defined coded value. For the variable data fields, the list gives the name of the indicator positions and any defined coded values and the name of the subfield codes and any defined coded values. For all variable fields, the **repeatability/nonrepeatability code** at the field level specifies whether the field may be repeated in a record. For variable data fields, the subfield repeatability code specifies whether the subfield code may be repeated within a field.

The **character position or field definition and scope** area describes the contents of the character position or field, the appropriateness of its use in specific kinds of bibliographic records, and gives other information, such as field repeatability in particular circumstances, the use of required lists or rules in formulating the data, etc.

The **guidelines for applying content designators** area describes the content and scope of each coded value, indicator, or subfield code and gives other information, such as appropriateness for use and repeatability in certain circumstances. The coded values and subfield codes in this area are presented in alphabetical/numerical order. Examples showing the use of the content designator are provided immediately following the description. The examples illustrate the application of specific MARC content designation. The data may be fuller or less full than would be used in actual cataloging practice. Most of the examples reflect the application of AACR 2 and ISBD; however, some reflect a generalized MARC application. Other examples illustrate specific points.

The **input conventions** area provides general guidance for the application of the content designators, and for such things as punctuation, spacing, and the use of display constants. The punctuation used within a field is generally dictated by descriptive cataloging or subject heading system/thesaurus rules. The input conventions clarify MARC punctuation practices especially with respect to final punctuation. In the discussion of punctuation practices, *mark of punctuation* is a period (.), a question mark (?), an exclamation mark (!), or a hyphen (-).

The **content designator history** area provides a record of significant content designator changes. The types of changes that are included are:

- * newly defined content designators that impact on coding consistency within a file, e.g., the location of a meeting entered under a corporate body was not separately subfield coded in the X10 fields prior to the definition of subfield $c in 1980.
- * redefined codes and values, e.g., in X10 fields, both the number and the name of a part/section of a work were contained in subfield $p prior to the redefinition of subfield $p for only the name of a part/section of a work in 1979.
- * changes in codes and values for consistency across MARC specifications, e.g., in 008/24-27 for the books specifications, code f (Handbooks) was identified by code h prior to 1979.
- * changes in repeatability when it impacts on file consistency, e.g., field 020 was not repeatable prior to 1977; multiple ISBN data were contained in repeatable subfields $a, $b, and $c.
- * restructuring, e.g., field 007 (Physical Description Fixed Field) in 1980.
- * obsolete content designation, e.g., subfield $b (Number) in the X11 fields when subfield $n was redefined to include meeting numbers in 1979. Obsolete content designation formerly defined in only one format are designated *[USMARC only]* or *[CAN/MARC only]*; unmarked items were defined in both formats.

In the MARC formats, a distinction is made between **obsolete** and **deleted** content designators. An **obsolete** content designator is one that may have been used in MARC records and that may continue to appear in records created prior to the date it was made obsolete. Obsolete content designators are not used in new records. An obsolete content designator is recorded in the *Content Designator History* area. Content designation instructions are provided for retrospective conversion of records having data elements that would have been identified by the obsolete content designator. A **deleted** content designator is not recorded in the history area and will no longer appear anywhere in the MARC documentation. A content designator that had been reserved in MARC but has not been defined, or one that had been defined but is known with near certainty not to have been used, may be deleted from the format. A deleted content designator is available for redefinition in a format. A deleted content designator is available for redefinition in a format.

Typographical Conventions

Throughout this document, the following typographical conventions are used:

* 0 - The graphic 0 represents the digit zero in tags, fixed-position character positions, indicator positions, and other places numerics are used. This character must be distinguished from an uppercase letter O in examples or text.
* # - The graphic symbol # is used for a blank in coded fields and in other special situations where the existence of the character blank might be ambiguous. (In most textual examples, the blank is represented in the conventional way, by the absence of a character.)
* $ - The graphic symbol $ is used for the delimiter portion of a subfield code. Within the text, subfield codes are referred to as *subfield $a*, for example.
* / - Specific character positions of the Leader, Directory, field 007, field 008 are expressed using a slash and the number of the character position, e.g., Leader/06, 007/00, 008/12.
* 1 - The graphic 1 represents the digit one (hex 31). This character must be distinguished from a lowercase roman alphabet letter l (hex 6C) and uppercase alphabetic letter I (hex 4C) in examples or text.

* | - The graphic | represents a fill character in MARC examples. When this mark appears in the left margin, it indicates areas of the text of this document where changes have been made.

STANDARDS AND OTHER DOCUMENTS RELATED TO THIS FORMAT

The *MARC 21 Format for Bibliographic Data* should be used with the following standards and related documentation. When a standard is applicable to data in specific fields of the format, the fields are given in brackets following the citation.

National and International Standards

ISO publications may be obtained from the International Organization for Standardization (ISO) and their agents; and ANSI/NISO Z39 publications may be obtained from the National Information Standards Organization (NISO).

* *Format for Information Exchange* (ISO 2709) and *Bibliographic Information Interchange* (ANSI/NISO Z39.2)
* *Code for the Representation of Names of Countries and their Subdivisions: Part 2, Country subdivision code* (ISO 3166-2)
* *International Standard Book Numbering (ISBN)* (ISO 2108)
* *International Standard Music Number (ISMN)* (ISO 10957)
* *International Standard Recording Code (ISRC)* (ISO 3901)
* *International Standard Serial Number (ISSN)* (ISO 3297) (ANSI/NISO Z39.9)
* *Representations of Dates and Times* (ISO 8601)
* *Serial Item and Contribution Identifier (SICI)* (ANSI/NISO Z39.56)
* *International Standard Technical Report Number (ISRN)* (ISO 10444) and *Standard Technical Report Number and Description* (ANSI/NISO Z39.23)

MARC Standards

* These publications are available from the Library of Congress, Cataloging Distribution Service, Washington, DC 20541, USA (Worldwide distribution) and Canadian Government Publishing - PWGSC, Ottawa, Ontario K1A 0S9, Canada (Canadian distribution).

USMARC Documentation

MARC 21 supersedes the 1994 edition of *USMARC Format for Bibliographic Data: Including Guidelines for Content Designation* and updates No. 1 (March 1995), No. 2 (March 1996), and No. 3 (July 1997) to that edition. With Update No.3 the USMARC and CAN/MARC formats were identical format specifications. The 1994 edition superseded the 1988 edition of the format and its four updates published between 1988 and 1991. The 1988 edition incorporated the base text of the 1980 edition published under the title *MARC Formats for Bibliographic Data* (MFBD) and the 15 updates to that edition published between 1980 and 1987. The 1980 edition was a compilation of separate MARC format documents developed for different types of material and published between 1969 and 1977.

CAN/MARC Documentation

MARC 21 supersedes the 1994 edition of *Canadian MARC Communication Format for Bibliographic Data* and its six updates published between 1994 and 1998. Update number six contained the changes to CAN/MARC required to align with USMARC. With this update, the specifications contained in the CAN/MARC and USMARC formats were identical. The 1994 edition superseded the 1988 edition and its seven updates issued between 1988 and 1991. The 1988 edition was produced by amalgamating separately issued CAN/MARC formats for monographs and serials.

2

MARC 21 : Fieldwise Examples

010 –800 VARIABLE DATE FIELDS

A field in the directory identifiles thes files . Thes part of the record contins the information we are familiar with from a catalogue card. Fields in this part are grouped in 'Levels For example the 100 – 130 fields contain the main entry. All variable fields can be repeated as many times as necessnry to accommodate multiple sub – fields; e.g. authors, etc. But many fields are not repeatable dut to the specific nature of cataloguing e.g. the main entry fields in the 100 level . Repeatable fields are indicated by an 'R' in the following section with the field name. The absence of 'R' indicated that the element is not repeatable and can only occur once in the record.

010 – 090 NUMBER AND CODES FIELDS

These fields contain control numbers, classification number, codes {language, etc.} and other related date. The following fields have been included in the NBD input sheet.

015	National Bibliography Database Catalogue
020	International Standard Book Number (ISBN)

040 Cataloguing Source

082 Dewey Decimal Classification Number

NATIONAL BIBLIOGRAPHY DATABASE CATALOG NUMBER

This field contains an eight - digit number, which is assigned by the central agency controlling the bibliographic records. The first two digits ir, the number indicate the year and rest serial number of the records prepared during the year. If the serial number [six digits] consists less than six digits the zeros should be placed before it to make it six digit number. Only one bibliographic record will be prepared for a set of multi-volume book. Therefore only one number will be assigned to it. In case the library received the first volume of a multi - volume book and rest will be received when published, assign the number to only first record. Because information about the rest of the volumes will only be updated in the record of the first volume. This number will be assigned centrally and agency preparing input sheet need not to fill this field.

Indicators φφ

Subfield No subfiled identifier

National Bibliography Number [Assigned by Controller]

Examples

015 φφ 7400381090

020 INTERNATIONAL STANDARD BOOK NUMBER [ISBN] [R]:

The ISBN is an unique assigned to a monographic publication by designate agencies in each country. This is a ten-digit number by which books and their corresponding MARC records can be identified. The final digit, which is a cheek- digit used to check the validity of number.

indicators φφ

Subfield

$a = International Standard Book Number (ISBN)

Examples

020	φφ	3527267700 (VCH, Weinheim)
020	φφ	8170230020 (set)
020	φφ	8170234697

040 CATALOGING SOURCE

This field is used to indicate the source of cataloguing. This code should be taken from the list of Codes for Libraries. This code will be entered only when the library is cataloguing the item originally, with no derived cataloguing.

Indicators φφ

Subfield

$a- Original cataloguing agency

Examples

040	φφ	PBPULP
040	φφ	TNIITS

041 LANGUAGE CODE

This field contains the codes for languages associated with the item being cataloged. This field is used when the language code given in field 008/ 35- 37 is insufficient to convey full information for a multilingual item or a translation.

INDICATORS

First Translation indication.

0 Item not a translation / does not include translation.

1 Item is or includes a translation .

Second φ

Subfields

$a- Language code of text or separate titles.

$h- Language code of original language/ or intermediate translation of text

(R)

Examples

041 1φ eng $a Kas

041 1φ engfreger

041 1φ eng $h fre (if the item is in English, translated from French)

082 DEWEY DECIMAL CLASSIFICATION NUMBER

This field contains the class number assigned by the NBD agency. This field is not used to enter the call/ class number that the local library assign to the items in its collection. This field will not be used by the libraries who are cataloguing the item originally. However, if the Dewey Decimal Class Number appears in CIP data of the item, the same can be entered by the library cataloguing the item originally.

Indicators φφ

Subfields

$a – Classification number

$2- Edition number

Examples

082 φφ 92294 $2 20

082 φφ 823$220

100 MAIN ENTRY – PERSONAL NAME

The person chiefly responsible for the certain of the intellectual or artistic content of the work. All the works of personal authorship should be entered in this field. It may be personal author, principal personal author or the probable personal author. In case of shared personal authorship and mixed personal authorship the person named firs should be entered.

Relaters, such as editors, illustrators are not entered in this field.

Indicators

First	Type of personal name.
0	Forename only
1	Single surname
2	Multiple surname
Second	φ

Subfields

$s- Personal name

$b- Numeration

$c- Title and other words associated with name (R)

$d- Dates associated with the name

$d- Fuller form of the name

Examples

100	0φ	Ram Gopal
100	0φ	John Paul $b 1, $c Pope
100	1φ	Tagore , Rabindranath, $d 1861-1941
100	1φ	Clapper, John $q (John samuel)
100	2φ	Das Gupta, Gobinda

110 MAIN ENTRY – CORPORATE NAME

A corporate name is an organization, association , institution, firm, government , agency or a group of persons that is identified by a particular name and that acts, or may act oas an entry.

Indicators

First	Type of corporate name
1	*Jurisdiction name*

(The name of a political jurisdiction used along with a period or followed by a qualifier)

2. Name in direct order

(May be an acronym or initials)

Second φ

Subfields

$a- Corporate name or jurisdiction name as entry element

$b- Subordinate unit (R)

$c- Location of meeting

$d- Date of meeting or treaty singing (R)

$n- Number of part/ section / meeting (R)

$p- Name of part/ section of a work (R)

Examples

110 1φ France

110 1φ Maxico City (Maxico)

110 1φ India. $b President

110 1φ United State $b Congress $n (87th, 2nd Session : $d 1962)

110 2φ International Labour Organization. $b European Regional Conference $n (2nd : 4d. 1968 : $c Geneva, Switzerland)

110 2φ SPIE.$b The International Society for Optical Engineering. $b Proceedings $d (1994 : $c Orlando, Florida)

111 MAIN ENTRY – MEETING NAME

Enter a work under name of conference , expedition , or event falling with the definition of corporate body, provided that they are prominently named in the item being catalogued.

If you enter a conference name indirectly (i.e., under the name of a corporate body), use field 110 . If in doubt , use this field.

Indicators

First : The form of name .

1 Jurisdiction name

(The name of a political jurisdiction used along with a period or followed by a qualifier)

2. Name in direct order

(May be an acronym or initials)

Second φ

Subfileds

$a- Meeting name or jurisdiction name as entry element

$c- Location of the meeting

$d- Date of meeting (R)

$e- Subordinate unit (R)

$n- Number of part/ section / meeting (R)

$p- Name of part/ section of a work (R)

Examples

111 2φ African Regional Symposium on Telematics for Development $d (1995 : $c Addis Ababa, Ethiopia)

111 2φ WSA ' 93 $N (3rd : $d 1993 : $c Italy)

130 – MAIN ENTRY – UNIFORM TITLE

Use uniform title as main entry heading if it item bears a title that differs from the uniform title. It is used to bring together records for the same item if different manifestations (e.g translations) appears under different titles. this field may be used for the following types of uniform titles.

a. Anonymous works

b. Treaties and inter – governmental agreement.

c. Composite manuscripts

If main entry field is 100, 110, or 111 then field 240 should be used to enter uniform title.

Indicators 0φ

Subfields

$a- Uniform title

$f- Date of a work

$k- Form subheading (R)

$l- Language of the work

$n- Number of part/ section / meeting (R)

$p- Name of part/ section of a work (R)

Examples

130 0φ Genesis (Anglo – saxon poem)

130 0φ Vedas, $p Rigveda

130 0φ Bible , $p. O.T $k Selections

130 0φ Vedas. $1 English.

240- UNIFORM TITLE

Uniform Title is used to identify an item if it has appeared under varying title. It may be in the form of personal, corporate, or meeting name. Uniform Title also provides identification for a work when the title by which it is known differs from the title proper of the item being catalogued.

Use field 130 for Uniform Title is the main entry.

Indicators 10

Sub-fields

$a- Uniform title

$f- Date of a work

$k- Form subheading (R)

$l- Language of the work

$n- Number of part/ section of a work (R)

$p- Name of part/ section of a work (R)

240 10 Arabian nights

240 10 Iliad

240 10 Genesis (Book of the Bible)

240 10 Poems. $p Selections

240 10 Correspondence. $p Selections.

245 TITLE STATEMENT

It is title proper, which may also include, reminder of title, other title information, and statement of responsibility / reminder of title page transcription . Title statement is the name by which an item known. Enter a period at the end of this field.

Indicators

First Title added entry.

0 No title added entry.

(Title is the main entry i.e. when there is no IXX field)

1 Title added entry

(Title added entry is required, when IXX field is present)

Second Non- filing characters.

0-9 Number of non- filing characters present

(Enter the number of characters in the articles, plus spaces, punctuation, and diacritics that precede first significant word Enter 0 if the title does not began with an article)

Sub-fields

$a- Title

$b-Reminder of the title (Subtitle or parallel title)

$c- Statement of responsibility

$n- Number of part/ section of work (R)

$p- Name of part/ section of a work (R)

Examples

245 00 Southeast Asia : $b past and present , / $c edited by [R.P. Mishra]

245 00 Progress in nuclear energy . $n Series 2, $p Reactors.

245 10 Unconventional / $c by Jack Wodford, Master Willium's clock/ by John Hagwood; illustrated by Robin Filiming.

245 10 Wood crec = $b Les Cris dcs formets

245 10 Selected poems / $c Rabindranath Tagore; translated by Willium Radice.

246 VARYING FORM OF TITLE (R)

This field is used for the further identification (added) of the item. We can use the varying form of the title appearing on different part of an item which differs significantly form the title contained in field 245 and if it helps to further identify the item.

This field is also used for title tracing portion of the item being catalogued.

Indicators

First

0 Note , on the title added entry

1 *(if you want to print field 246 as a note, but not as a title added entry)*

1. Note, title added entry

(if you want to print field 246 as a note, and as a title added entry)

3. No note, title added entry

(if you want to print field 246 as a title added entry but not as a note)

Second

φ No information provided.

0 Portion of title. Any portion of the full title (except parallel titles) requited.

1 Parallel title (contained in subfiled $b of 245)

2 Distinctive title (special title in addition to regular title)

3 Other title (title appeared on item seems to be more appropriate)

4 Cover title (title printed on original cover of publication)

5 Added title page title (A title in another language, if any)

6 Caption title (A title printed at the head of the first page of text)

7 Running title (A title printed at the top or bottom margin of each page of a publication)

8 Spine title (title found on the spine of publication)

Sub-fields

$a – Title proper / short title

$b – Subtitle

$f – Volume / issue numbers and / or date of work

$n – Number of part / section of work (R)

$p – Name of part / section of a work (R)

Examples

246 30 Beauty and the beast

246 31 Nihon

246 12 Campus planning

246 30 Modern writing

246 10 Encyclopedia of science and technology

246 30 Sivananda Vilasa

250 EDITION STATEMENT

This field contains information regarding edition statement as found on the item. Use standard abbreviations as per AACR – 2. An edition statement may include a personal name. If the edition statement consists of characters that are neither numeric nor alphanumeric, enter the statement in words in the language and script of the title proper and enclose them in square bracket. If the edition statement consists of a letter or letters and / or a number or numbers without accompanying words, add an appropriate word or abbreviation in square brackets.

Indicators φφ

Sub fields

$a – Edition statement

$b – Remainder of edition statement

Examples

250 φφ 1st ed., rev. impression

250 φφ 2nd ed., rev. and enl. / $b by W. Chalmer

260 IMPRINT (PUBLICATION, DISTRIBUTION, ETC.)

This field contains all information about the place of publication, name of publishers / distributors, date of publication, of the item being catalogued.

Indicators φφ

Sub fields

$a – Place of publication (R)

$b – Name of publisher (R)

$c – Date of publication (R)

Examples

260 φφ New York : $b John Wiley, $c c1992.

260 φφ [U.S.A.] : $b international publishers, $c 1968

260 φφ [s.1. : $b s.n.]

260 φφ Weinheim ; $a New York : $b VCH, $c c1989

300 PHYSICAL DESCRIPTION (R)

It includes physical description of item, about its extent, dimension s, and form. If given item is available in different formats, give the physical description of the format in hand.

Indicators φφ

Sub fields

$a – Pagination (R)

$b – Illustrations, etc.

$c – Dimensions

$e – Accompanying material

Examples

300 φφ xviii, 323 p, ; $b maps, ports

300 φφ 3 v. ; $c 24 – 28 cm.

300 φφ 8 v. in 5 $b ill. ; $c 75mm.

300 φφ v. < 4 > : $b ill. ; $c 25cm.

440 SERIES STATEMENT / ADDED ENTRY – TITLE (R)

If an item is one of a series, give its title proper of the series. This field is used for series statements in tracing for a series under title. The content of this field is also used as a series added entry. Enter all initial articles appearing in the series statement and use indicator 2 for appropriate non-filling characters. Do not enter parenthesis enclosing the series statement. Do not enter spaces between the initials appear in the field, whether separated or not separated by periods.Enter multiple series statements separately, in which they appear in catalogue record.

Indicators

First φ

Second Non-filling characters

0 – 9 number of Non-filling characters present (Enter the number of characters in the

articles, plus spaces, punctuation, and diacritics that precede first significant word Enter 0 if the title does not begin with an article)

Sub-fields

$a – Title of series

$n – Number of part / section of a work ®

$p – Name of part / section of a work ®

$v – Volume number / sequential designation

$x – ISSN

Examples

440 φ0 Lecture notes in computer science $v 724

440 φ0 Music for today. $n series 2

440 φ0 This is America; $v no. 1

440 φ4 The British Travel series, $x ISSN 002-5654

440 φ0 Classics of the East

500 GENERAL NOTE (R)

This field is used for any note for which there is not a defined field in the bibliographic record.

Indicators φφ

Sub-field

$a – General note

Examples

500 φφ Original signed by John Hancock.

500 φφ Previously published as : Penter Psmith

500 φφ Previous ed.: Harmondsworth : Penguin, 1950

500 φφ Published simultaneously in India

500 φφ "S.R. Dongerkey, Chairman"

500 φφ Fiction

500 φφ Autobiography

500 φφ Novel

500 φφ On p. opposite t.p. : United Nations Centre of Regional Development

500 φφ On t.p verso : Proceedings of the NATO . Advanced Study Institute on Laser Applications to Chemistry , held June 27-July 11, 1982, at San Miniato, Italy.

504 BIBLIOGRAPHY, ETC . NOTE (R)

This field contains the notes about the bibliography , Discography. And/or other bibliographic note . reverences of an item. Use this field when the presence of an index is also mentioned in bibliography note. Use field 500 when only a note about index is entered.

Indicators φφ

Sub-field

$a – Bibliography, etc. note

Examples

504 φφ Includes bibliographical references and index.

504 φφ Includes bibliographical references (p. 310-325).

505 FORMATED CONTENTS NOTE (R)

Contents note contain the titles of separate works or parts of an item. Can also includes statement of responsibility, volume number or other designations. Enhanced content note should be entered in the subfiled. The field is used for formal content note.

Indicators φφ

First Type of contents notes.

0 Complete contents

(The entire item is in hand and described at the note)

1. Incomplete contents

(The entire item is not in hand and the note descried only what is available)

2. Partial contents

(The entire item is in hand, but the note describes only selected parts of the item)

Second 0

Subfield

$a- Formatted contents note

Examples

505 00 v. 1. An overview / R.P Mishra ; with contribution from Moonis Raza, T.R. Laxmanan, and Raanan Weitz—v. 2 Brazil and Nigeria/ Bertha K. Becker, Akin L. Manogunije—v. Indonesia and the Philippines / Mubyrto... [et al]...v.4 India and Bangladesh/ K.V. Sundram, S.N Mishra , Taherul Islam - v.5. China and Tanzania / Chung- Tong WU, David F. Lp, J.H.L. Media.

505 10 v. 4 Thermal sensor

505 10 v.3 stone culture and Indus vally civilization.

505 00 v.1. Raja Ram Mohan Roy –v.2 Golpark Krishan Gokhle— v.3 Mahadev Ranade—v.4 Bal Gangadhar Tilak —v.5. M.N Roy - v.6 Subhash Chandra Bose—v. 7 M.K. Gandhi—v.8 Jayaprakash Narayan—v.9 Rammanohar Lohia—v. 10 Jawaharlal Nehru

546 LANGUAGE NOTE (R)

Note about language of the text is entered in this field

Indicators φφ

$a- Language note.

Examples

041 0 engfreger

546 φφ Text in English and French each with special tp and separate paging.

600 SUBJECT ADDED ENTRY – PERSONAL NAME (R)

Added entry provides access to additional to that of main entry heading. Here the subject added entry is made when the entry element (subject) is a personal name.

Indicators

First Type of personal name.

0 Forename

1 Single surname

2 Multiple surname

Second 0

Subfields

$a- Personal name

$b- Numeration

$c- Title and other words associated with a name (R)

$d- Dates associates with a name

$n- Number of part/ section of work (R)

$p- Name of part/ section of a work (R)

$t- Title of a work

$q- Fuller form of name

$x- General subdivision (R)

$y- Chronological subdivision (R)

$z- Geographical subdivision (R)

Examples

600	10	Roy , Raja Ram Mohan
600	10	Dark, Francis, $d 1540? - 1596
600	10	Shakespeare, William , $x History $y 18th century
600	10	Ford, Gerald R, $d 1913- $x Museums, relies etc. $z Michigan

610 SUBJECT ADDED ENTRY- CORPORATE NAME (R)

A subject added entry in which entry element is corporate name. It may be name of association, institution, business firm, non- profit enterprises, government , agencies. This field is used for locally assigned corporate name subject heading as well as subject authority assigned entries.

Indicators

First Type of corporate name.

1 Jurisdiction name

2 Name in direct order

Second 0

Subfields

$a- Corporate name or jurisdiction name as entry element

$b- Subordinate unit (R)

$c- Location of meeting

$d- Date of meeting or treaty signing

$n- Number of part/ section / meeting (R)

$p- Name of part/ section of a work (R)

$t- Title of a work

$q- Fuller form of name

$y- Chronological subdivision (R)

$z- Geographical subdivision (R)

Examples

610	20	Dauters of the American Revolution. $b Mary clap Wooster Chapter (new Heaven, Conv.)
610	20	Dauters of the American Revolution. $b Mary clap wooster Chapter (new Heaven, Conv) $c. London
610	10	United States, $d 1974 Nov. 19.

611- SUBJECT ADDED ENTRY- MEETING NAME (R)

This field contains the meeting name used as subject added entry. These can be names of conferences, exhibitions contents etc,. if the name of conference, meeting is entered directly i.e. under the name of a corporate body, use field 610. In case of any doubt use only this field.

Indicator 20

Subfields

$a- Meeting name or jurisdiction name as entry element

$c- Location of meeting

$d- Date of meeting (R)

$e- Subordinate unit (R)

$p- Name of part/ section of a work (R)

$t- Title of a work

$x- General subdivision (R)

$y- Chronological subdivision (R)

$z- Geographical subdivision (R)

Examples

611	20	Salon (Exhibition : Paris , France)
611	20	Epson Derby , England (Horse race) $x. History $y 20th century
611	20	Olympic Games $n (23rd : $d 1984 : $c Los Angeles calif.) $v Maps

630 SUBJECT ADDED ENTRY – UNIFORM TITLE (R)

This field is used for uniform title used as subject added entries. It is used to bring together the records of the item when appear under different titles.

Indicators φ0

Sub fields

$a – Uniform title

$f – Date of work

$k – Form subheading

$l – Language of work

$x – General subdivision (R)

$y – Chronological subdivision (R)

$z – Geographic subdivision (R)

Examples

630	φ0	Ten Commandments $x False witness
630	φ0	Arabian nights $x History $y 20th century
630	φ0	Koran $x Publication and distribution $z Saudi Arabia
630	φ0	Bhagvadgita $n Criticism, interpretation.
630	φ0	Bible. $k Manuscripts. $p N.T.

650 SUBJECT ADDED ENTRY – TOPICAL HEADING (R)

Topical term used as a subject added entry is entered in this field. This field is used for topical subject added entries and other subject added entries not entered in fields 600 – 630 or 651. This field should be used for the following types of topical subject entries:

(a) General terms (e.g. Dogs, Chemistry)

(b) Systematic names of families, species in botany and zoology and chemical compounds.

(c) Names of events and holidays.

(d) Names of terms applied to individual objects or classes of objects (e.g. universities, colleges, etc.)

Indicators φ0

Sub fields

$a – Topical term or geographical name as entry element

$x – General subdivision (R)

$y – Chronological subdivision (R)

$z – Geographic subdivision (R)

Examples

650 φ0 Rural development

650 φ0 Science $x Encyclopedias

650 φ0 Universities and colleges $x Examination

650 φ0 Koran $x Biography

650 φ0 Physics $x Encyclopedias

650 φ0 Presidents $z India $x Biography.

651 SUBJECT ADDED ENTRY – GEOGRAPHIC NAME (R)

Enter geographic name used as subject added entry in this field. They may include natural features, celestial bodies, Archaeological sites, or any other geographic entries.

Indicators φ0

Sub fields

$a – Geographic name.

$x – General subdivision (R)

$y – Chronological subdivision (R)

$z – Geographic subdivision (R)

Examples

651 φ0 India $x Encyclopedias.

651 φ0 Asia, Southeastern $x History.

651 φ0 Alaska $x History $y To 1867

651 φ0 Japan $x Foreign relations $z Korea (South)

651 φ0 India $x Politics and government $y 1977

653 UNCONTROLLED INDEX TERMS (R)

Enter the subjects terms used as subject added entries that are self constructed i.e. not derived from controlled subject heading list e.g. Library of Congress Subject Headings.

Indicators φφ

Sub fields

$a – Uncontrolled term

Examples

653 φφ Ocean

653 φφ Bed

653 φφ Soils

700 ADDED ENTRY – PERSONAL NAME (R)

Enter personal name which is used as added entry element in this field. It may be forename, surname, or any other form of personal name.

Use this field to enter following types of personal names as added entries:

* Shared authorship
* Collaborators
* Editors and compilers
* Analytical works

Indicators Type of personal name entry element

First Type of personal name

0 Forename

1 Single surname

2 Multiple surname

Second Type of added entry

φ	No information provided
2	Analytical entry

Sub fields

$a – Personal name

$b – Numeration

$c – Title and other words

$d – Dates associated with the name

$n – Number of part / section of a work (R)

$p – Name of part / section of work (R)

$t – Title of a work

Examples

700	1φ	Aptheker, Herbert
700	1φ	Evans, Montgomeny $b II
700	1φ	E. Sheila $q (Escovedo), $d 1939
700	1φ	Hindemith, Paul, $d 1895-1963
700	1φ	Cohen, J.M.
700	1φ	Hagwod, John. $t Master Williun's Clock

710 ADDED ENTRY – CORPORATE NAME (R)

Entry corporate name which is used as added entry in this field. It may include name of associations, institutions, business firms etc.

Indicators

First	Type of corporate name
1	Jurisdiction name
2	Name in direct order
Second	Type of added entry
1	No information provided
2	Analytical entry

Sub fields

$a – Corporate name or jurisdiction name as entry element

$b – Subordinate unit (R)

$c – Location of meeting

$d – Date of meeting or treaty signing (R)

$n – Number of part / section / meeting (R)

$p – Name of part / section of a work (R)

$t – Title of a work

Examples

710	22	Catholic church
710	22	Catholic church. $b Pope (1958-1963: John XXIII)
710	1φ	Algeria. $d 1682 Apr. 20.
710	1φ	United States. $t Constitution. $p 13th Amendment
710	12	Philippines. $t Labour code of the Philippines

711 ADDED ENTRY – MEETING NAME (R)

Enter the meeting name used as added entry element in this field. It may be the name of conferences, meetings, exhibitions, festivals etc.

Indicators

First	2
Second	Type of added entry
φ	No information provided
2	Analytical entry

Sub fields

$a – Meeting name or jurisdiction name as entry element

$c – Location of meeting

$d – Date of meeting

$e – Subordinate unit (R)

$n – Number of part / section / meeting (R)

$p – Name of part / section of a work (R)

$t – Title of a work

Examples

711 2φ Conference on philosophy and its history $d (1983 : $c University of Lancaster)

711 2φ Olympic games. $n (21st : $d 1976: $c Montreal, Quebec)

711 2φ Mostly Mozart Festival $c Orchestra.

711 2φ International conference on Gnosticism

711 2φ Asian Games $n (9th : $d 1982: $c Delhi, India)

730 ADDED ENTRY – UNIFORM TITLE (R)

The entry element of the added entry is a uniform title. It is used for same work which appear under different title.

Indicators

First 0

Second Type of added entry

φ No information provided

2 Analytical entry

Sub fields

$a – Uniform title

$f – Date of a work

$k – Form subheading (R)

$l – Language of a work

$n – Number of part / section / meeting (R)

$p – Name of part / section of a work (R)

$t – Title of a work

Examples

730 0φ Treaty of Utrecht

730 02 Talmud. $k Selections.

740 ADDED ENTRY – VARIANT TITLE (R)

An added entry in which the entry element is a title that is different from the title proper portion of field 245.

Indicators

First 0

Second Type of added entry

φ No information provided

2 Analytical entry

Sub fields

$a – Uncontrolled related / analytical title

$n – Number of part / section / meeting (R)

$p – Name of part / section of a work (R)

Examples

740 02 I want to tell you.

850 HOLDINGS LIBRARY (R)

Enter the holding details of an item in this field.

Indicators

First Type of item

0 Not a multi-volume item.

1 Multi volume items where all volumes are held.

2 Part of a multi-volume item.

Second ILL availability

0 Not for Inter Library Loan

1 For Inter Library Loan

Sub fields

$a – Library code

$b – Volumes held

$n – Local Call No.

$p – Local Accession No.

Examples

850	01	DLIIC $n 968.06
		BUR $p 18878.
850	10	DLIIC $b 1.4 $n 954.3 KAU $p 15678-81

MARC21: BIBLIOGRAPHIC FORMAT

LEADER (M):

Record Status	Type of record	Bibliographical level	Descriptive Catg.Form

....

CONTROL FIELD-MONOGRAPH & SERIAL (008)

Type of Date	Date1	Date2	Place of Publ.	Illustration	Target Audience

Form Of Item	Nature of Contents	Govt. Pub.	Conf. Pub.	Festschrift	Index	Undefined	Literary Form

Biography	Language	Modified Record	Cata. Source

....

NAME OF THE FIELD INCL. MARC21 TAG	INDICATORS 1	2	DATA WITH SUBFIELD IDENTIFIERS
ISBN NO. (020) (R)	#	#	$a ISBN NO. (NR) $c Terms of Availability, i.e. Price (NR)
ISSN (022) (R)	#0-serial of Inter-International interest 1-serial not of International interest	#	$a International Standard Serial No. (NR)
DEWEY DECIMAL CLASSIFICATION NUMBER (082) (R)	0-full edition 1-abridged ed.	#	$a Classification No. (R) $b2 Edition number (NR) (for unprocessed book only)
MAIN ENTRY-PERSONAL NAME (100) (NR)	0-Fore-name 1-Surname 3-Family name	#—Undefined	$a Personal name (NR) $b Numeration (NR) $c Title and other words as. with a name(R)
MAIN ENTRY – CORPORATE NAME (110) NR	0-Inverted name I-Jurisdictionname 2 – Name in direct order	#Undefined	$a Corporate name (NR) $b Subordinate unit (R) $c Location of meeting (NR) $Date of meeting ® $n No of Part/section/meeting.

MAIN ENTRY – MEETING name (111) (NR)	0-Inverted name I-Jurisdictionname 2 – Name in direct order	#Undefined	$a Meeting name (NR) $c Location of meeting (NR) $d Date of Meeting (NR) $e Subordinate unit (R) $n Number of part/section/meting (R)
MAIN ENTRY - UNIFORM TITLE (130) (NR)	0-9 – no filling character	#	$a Uniform title (NR) $d Date of treaty signing (R) $k Form subheading ® $l language of work (NR) $n Number of part/section ®
TITLA STATEMENT (245) (NR)	0 – No added entry 1 – Added entry	0-9 No. of non-filing character	$a Title (NR) $b Reminder of title (NR) $c Statement of responsibility (NR)
EDITION STATEMENT (250) (nr)	#	#	$a Edition statement (NR) $b Reminder of edition statement (NR)
PUBLICATION DIST. ETC.(260) ®	# -Not applicable 2 – Inter vending publisher 3-Current latest pub.	#	$a Place of publication ® $b Name of publisher (@) $c Date of Publication.
PHYSICAL DESC. (300) ®	#	#	$a Extent ® $bother physical details (NR) $c Dimensions ®

			$e Accompanying material (NR)
SERIES STATEMENT/ ADDED ENTRY-TITLE (440) (R)	#	0-9Number of Non-filing character	$a Title (NR) $n No. of part/section of a work
SERIES STATEMENT (490)(R)	0 – Series not traced 1 – Series traced differently	#	$a Series statement ®
GENERAL NOTE (500) (R)	#	#	$a General note (NR)
CONTENTS NOTE (505)(R)	0 Contents 1 – Incomplete contents 2 – Partial contents	# - basic 0 - Enhanced	$a Formated contents note (with punctuation of AACR-2) (NR)
SUBJECT ADDED ENTRY- PERSONAL NAME (600) (R)	0 – Fore-name 1 - Surname 3 – Family name	0-LCSH	$a Personal name (NR) $b Numeration (NR) $c Titles and other words asso. With name(R)
SUBJECT ADDED ENTRY- CORPORATE NAME (610) (R)	0 – Inverted name 1 – Jurisdiction name 2 – Name in direct order	0-LCSH	$a Meeting name (NR) $c Location of meeting (NR) $d Date of meeting (NR)
SUBJECT ADDED ENTRY- TOPICAL NAME (650) (R)	# - No Informa-tion provided 0 – No level specified 1 – Primary	0-LCSH	$a Topical term (NR) $v Form subdivision (R) $x General subdivision (R)

	2 - Secondary		$y Chronological subdivision (R) $z Geographic subdivision (R)
SUBJECT ADDED ENTRY- GEOGRAPHIC NAME (651) (R)	#	0-LCSH	$a Geographic name (NR) $v Form subdivision (R)
ADDED ENTRY- PERSONAL NAME (700) (R)	0 – Forename 1 – Surname 3 – Family name	#2 – Analy - tical entry	$a Personal name (NR) $b Numeration (NR) $c Titles and other words asso. with name.
ADDED ENTRY- CORPORATE NAME (710) (R)	0 – Inverted name 1 – Jurisdiction name 2- Name in direct order	#2- Analy -tical entry	$aCorporate name (NR) $b Subordinate unit ® $c Location of meeting (NR) $d Date of meeting (R)
ADDED ENTRY- MEETING NAME (711 (R)	0 – Inverted name 1 – Jurisdiction name 2- Name in direct order	#2- Analy- tical entry	$a Meeting name (NR) $c Location of meeting (NR) $d Date of meeting (NR)
ADDED ENTRY – UNIFORM TITLE (730) (R)	0-9 – Number of non- filing character	#2 – Analy- tical entry	$a Uniform title (NR)
LOCATION (852)	#1 – DDC8 – Other scheme	#	$allocation (NR)
ACCESSION NO. INCL. DT. (901)			$a Acc. No. $b Date of Acc.

	$c Bar code No.
CALL NO. (902)	$a Call No including author mark and individualization
SUBJECT HEADING DEFINED BY (903)	$a
ENTERED BY (904)	$a
VERIFIED BY (905)	$a

NB. #= Put blank. R means Repeatable. NR means Not Repeatable

3

MARC 21: Bibliographic Format of Periodicals

EXAMPLE 1

Journal of International development

Wiley Interscience
USA
November 2006

O.I.—Vol.18, no.8/November 2006/Bimonthly/Subject: Economics/ISSN: 0964-1748

MARC21: BIBLIOGRAPHIC FORMAT

LEADER (M):

Record Status	Type of record	Bibliographical level	Descriptive Catg.Form
n	a	s	a

CONTROL FIELD –MONOGRAPH & SERIAL (008)

Type of Date	Date1	Date2	Place of Publ.	Illustration	Target Audience
t	2006		us#	a	f

Form Of Item	Nature of Contents	Govt. Pub.	Conf. Pub.	Festschrift	Index	Undefined	Literary Form
#					1	#	

Biography	Language	Modified Record	Cata. Source
	eng	#	

NAME OF THE FIELD INCL. MARC21 TAG	INDICATORS 1	2	DATA WITH SUBFIELD IDENTIFIERS
ISBN NO. (020) (R)	#	#	ac 320.00
ISSN (022) (R)	#	#	$a 0954-1748
DEWEY DECIMAL CLASSIFICATION NUMBER (082) (R)	0	#	$a 330.5 $b 20th ed
MAIN ENTRY-PERSONAL NAME (100) (NR)			$a $b $c
MAIN ENTRY – CORPORATE NAME (110) NR			$a $b $c $d $n
MAIN ENTRY – MEETING name (111) (NR)			$a $c $d $e $n
MAIN ENTRY - UNIFORM TITLE (130) (NR)			$a $d $k $l $n
KEY TITLE(222)	#		$a Journal of international development $b
TITLE STATEMENT (245) (NR)			$a
EDITION STATEMENT (250) (nr)	#	#	$a
PUBLICATION DIST. ETC.(260) ®	3	#	$a USA $b Wiley Inter science

			$c 2006(Nov.)
PHYSICAL DESC. (300) ®	#	#	$a V.18,no.8 $b $c $e
SERIES STATEMENT/ ADDED ENTRY-TITLE (440) (R)	#		$a
SERIES STATEMENT (490)(R)			$a
GENERAL NOTE (500) (R)	#	#	$a Bimonthly
CONTENTS NOTE (505)(R)			$a
SUBJECT ADDED ENTRY- PERSONAL NAME (600) (R)			$a $b $c
SUBJECT ADDED ENTRY- CORPORATE NAME (610) (R)			$a $c $d
SUBJECT ADDED ENTRY- TOPICAL NAME (650) (R)	#	0	$a Economics $v Periodical $x $y $z
SUBJECT ADDED ENTRY- GEOGRAPHIC NAME (651) (R)			$a $v
ADDED ENTRY- PERSONAL NAME (700) (R)			$a $b $c
ADDED ENTRY- CORPORATE NAME (710) (R)			$a $b $c $d

ADDED ENTRY- MEETING NAME (711 (R)			$a $c $d
ADDED ENTRY – UNIFORM TITLE (730) (R)			$a
LOCATION (852)	1	#	$a
ACCESSION NO. INCL. DT. (901)			$a 1 $b 24.03.07 $c
CALL NO. (902)			$a 330.5JID
SUBJECT HEADING DEFINED BY (			$a S.Das
ENTERED BY (904)			$a S.Das
VERIFIED BY (905)			$a S.Das

NB. #= Put blank. R means Repeatable. NR means Not Repeatable

EXAMPLE 2

Bulletin of Material Science

Indian Academy of Sciences
Bangalore
December 2003

O.I.– Vol. 23, no. 7,December 2003/
Subject: Material science/ ISSN: 0250-4707

MARC21: BIBLIOGRAPHIC FORMAT

LEADER (M):

Record Status	Type of record	Bibliographical level	Descriptive Catg.Form
n	a	s	a

....

CONTROL FIELD- MONOGRAPH & SERIAL (008)

Type of Date	Date1	Date2	Place of Publ.	Illustration	Target Audience
t	2 0 0 3		b a i	a	f

Form Of Item	Nature of Contents	Govt. Pub.	Conf. Pub.	Festschrift	Index	Undefined	Literary Form
#					1	#	

Biography	Language	Modified Record	Cata. Source
	e n g	#	

....

NAME OF THE FIELD INCL. MARC21 TAG	INDICATORS 1	2	DATA WITH SUBFIELD IDENTIFIERS
ISBN NO. (020) (R)	#	#	$a $c 350.00
ISSN (022) (R)	#	#	$a 0250-4707
DEWEY DECIMAL CLASSIFICATION NUMBER (082) (R)	0	#	$a 551.05 $b 20th ed
MAIN ENTRY-PERSONAL NAME (100) (NR)			$a $b $c
MAIN ENTRY – CORPORATE NAME (110) NR			$a $b $c $d $n
MAIN ENTRY – MEETING name (111) (NR)			$a $c $d $e $n
MAIN ENTRY - UNIFORM TITLE (130) (NR)			$a $d $k $l $n
KEY TITLE(222)	#		$a Bulletin of material science $b
TITLE STATEMENT (245) (NR)			$a
EDITION STATEMENT (250) (nr)	#	#	$a
PUBLICATION DIST. ETC.(260) ®	3	#	$a Bangalore $b Indian Academy of Science

			$c 2003(Dec.)
PHYSICAL DESC. (300) ®	#	#	$a V.26,no.7 $b $c $e
SERIES STATEMENT/ ADDED ENTRY-TITLE (440) (R)	#		$a
SERIES STATEMENT (490)(R)			$a
GENERAL NOTE (500) (R)	#	#	$a
CONTENTS NOTE (505)(R)			$a
SUBJECT ADDED ENTRY- PERSONAL NAME (600) (R)			$a $b $c
SUBJECT ADDED ENTRY- CORPORATE NAME (610) (R)			$a $c $d
SUBJECT ADDED ENTRY- TOPICAL NAME (650) (R)	#	0	$a Material science $v Periodical $x $y $z
SUBJECT ADDED ENTRY- GEOGRAPHIC NAME (651) (R)			$a $v
ADDED ENTRY- PERSONAL NAME (700) (R)			$a $b $c
ADDED ENTRY- CORPORATE NAME (710) (R)			$a $b $c $d

ADDED ENTRY- MEETING NAME (711 (R)			$a $c $d
ADDED ENTRY – UNIFORM TITLE (730) (R)			$a
LOCATION (852)	1	#	$a
ACCESSION NO. INCL. DT. (901)			$a 2$b 24.03.07 $c
CALL NO. (902)			$a 551.05P03
SUBJECT HEADING DEFINED BY (			$a S.Das
ENTERED BY (904)			$a S.Das
VERIFIED BY (905)			$a S.Das

NB. #= Put blank. R means Repeatable. NR means Not Repeatable

EXAMPLE 3

Journal of Scientific & Industrial Research

National Institute of Science Communication And
Information Resources, CSIR
New Delhi
November 2006

O.I.– Vol. 65, no. 11, November 2006/ Monthly/ Subject: Scientific research, Industrial research / ISSN: 0022-4456

MARC21: BIBLIOGRAPHIC FORMAT

LEADER (M):

Record Status	Type of record	Bibliographical level	Descriptive Catg.Form
n	a	s	a

CONTROL FIELD –MONOGRAPH & SERIAL (008)

Type of Date	Date1	Date2	Place of Publ.	Illustration	Target Audience
t	2 0 0 6		n d i	a	f

Form Of Item	Nature of Contents	Govt. Pub.	Conf. Pub.	Festschrift	Index	Undefined	Literary Form
#					1	#	

Biography	Language	Modified Record	Cata. Source
	e n g	#	

NAME OF THE FIELD INCL. MARC21 TAG	INDICATORS 1	2	DATA WITH SUBFIELD IDENTIFIERS
ISBN NO. (020) (R)	#	#	$a $c 500.00
ISSN (022) (R)	#	#	$a 0022-4456
DEWEY DECIMAL CLASSIFICATION NUMBER (082) (R)	0	#	$a 607.205 $b 20th ed
MAIN ENTRY-PERSONAL NAME (100) (NR)			$a $b $c
MAIN ENTRY – CORPORATE NAME (110) NR			$a $b $c $d $n
MAIN ENTRY – MEETING name (111) (NR)			$a $c $d $e $n
MAIN ENTRY - UNIFORM TITLE (130) (NR)			$a $d $k $l $n
KEY TITLE(222)	#		$a Journal of scientific and industrial research $b
TITLE STATEMENT (245) (NR)			$a
EDITION STATEMENT (250) (nr)	#	#	$a
PUBLICATION DIST.	3	#	$a New Delhi

ETC.(260) ®			$b National Institute of science Communication And Information Resources, CSIR $c 2006(Nov.)
PHYSICAL DESC. (300) ®	#	#	$aV.65,no.11 $b $c $e
SERIES STATEMENT/ ADDED ENTRY-TITLE (440) (R)	#		$a
SERIES STATEMENT (490)(R)			$a
GENERAL NOTE (500) (R)	#	#	$a Monthly
CONTENTS NOTE (505)(R)			$a
SUBJECT ADDED ENTRY- PERSONAL NAME (600) (R)			$a $b $c
SUBJECT ADDED ENTRY- CORPORATE NAME (610) (R)			$a $c $d
SUBJECT ADDED ENTRY- TOPICAL NAME (650) (R)	#	0	$a Scientific research, Industrial research $v Periodical $x $y $z
SUBJECT ADDED ENTRY- GEOGRAPHIC NAME (651) (R)			$a $v
ADDED ENTRY- PERSONAL NAME (700) (R)			$a $b $c

ADDED ENTRY- CORPORATE NAME (710) (R)			$a $b $c $d
ADDED ENTRY- MEETING NAME (711 (R)			$a $c $d
ADDED ENTRY – UNIFORM TITLE (730) (R)			$a
LOCATION (852)	1	#	$a
ACCESSION NO. INCL. DT. (901)			$a 3 $b 24.03.07 $c
CALL NO. (902)			$a 607.205P06
SUBJECT HEADING DEFINED BY (			$a S.Das
ENTERED BY (904)			$a S.Das
VERIFIED BY (905)			$a S.Das

NB. #= Put blank. R means Repeatable. NR means Not Repeatable

EXAMPLE 4

The Journal of Academic Librarianship

Elsevier

U.S.A.

November 2006

O.I.– Vol. 22, no. 6, November 2006/ Bimonthly/

Subject: Library science/

ISSN: 0099-1333

MARC21: BIBLIOGRAPHIC FORMAT

LEADER (M):

n	a	s	a
Record Status	Type of record	Bibliographical level	Descriptive Catg.Form

....

CONTROL FIELD- MONOGRAPH & SERIAL (008)

t	2 0 0 6		u s #	a	f
Type of Date	Date1	Date2	Place of Publ.	Illustration	Target Audience

#					1	#	
Form Of Item	Nature of Contents	Govt. Pub.	Conf. Pub.	Festschrift	Index	Undefined	Literary Form

	e n g	#	
Biography	Language	Modified Record	Cata. Source

....

NAME OF THE FIELD INCL. MARC21 TAG	INDICATORS 1	2	DATA WITH SUBFIELD IDENTIFIERS
ISBN NO. (020) (R)	#	#	$a $c 175.00
ISSN (022) (R)	#	#	$a 0099-1333
DEWEY DECIMAL CLASSIFICATION NUMBER (082) (R)	0	#	$a 020.505 $b 20th ed
MAIN ENTRY-PERSONAL NAME (100) (NR)			$a $b $c
MAIN ENTRY – CORPORATE NAME (110) NR			$a $b $c $d $n
MAIN ENTRY – MEETING name (111) (NR)			$a $c $d $e $n
MAIN ENTRY - UNIFORM TITLE (130) (NR)			$a $d $k $l $n
KEY TITLE(222)	#		$a Journal of academic librarianship $b
TITLE STATEMENT (245) (NR)			$a
EDITION STATEMENT (250) (nr)	#	#	$a
PUBLICATION DIST.	3	#	$a USA

ETC.(260) ®			$b Elsevier $c 2006(Nov.)
PHYSICAL DESC. (300) ®	#	#	$a V.22,no.6 $b $c $e
SERIES STATEMENT/ ADDED ENTRY-TITLE (440) (R)	#		$a
SERIES STATEMENT (490)(R)			$a
GENERAL NOTE (500) (R)	#	#	$a Bimonthly
CONTENTS NOTE (505)(R)			$a
SUBJECT ADDED ENTRY- PERSONAL NAME (600) (R)			$a $b $c
SUBJECT ADDED ENTRY- CORPORATE NAME (610) (R)			$a $c $d
SUBJECT ADDED ENTRY- TOPICAL NAME (650) (R)	#	0	$a Library science $v Periodical $x $y $z
SUBJECT ADDED ENTRY- GEOGRAPHIC NAME (651) (R)			$a $v
ADDED ENTRY- PERSONAL NAME (700) (R)			$a $b $c
ADDED ENTRY- CORPORATE NAME (710) (R)			$a $b $c $d

ADDED ENTRY- MEETING NAME (711 (R)			$a $c $d
ADDED ENTRY – UNIFORM TITLE (730) (R)			$a
LOCATION (852)	1	#	$a
ACCESSION NO. INCL. DT. (901)			$a 4 $b 24.03.07 $c
CALL NO. (902)			$a 020.505P06
SUBJECT HEADING DEFINED BY (			$a S.Das
ENTERED BY (904)			$a S.Das
VERIFIED BY (905)			$a S.Das

NB. #= Put blank. R means Repeatable. NR means Not Repeatable

EXAMPLE 5

Journal of Light wave technology

Institute of Electrical and Electronics Engineers (IEEE)

New York

May 2005

O.I.– Vol. 23, no. 5, May 2005/ Monthly/

Subject: Light wave technology/

ISSN: 0733- 8724

MARC21: BIBLIOGRAPHIC FORMAT

LEADER (M):

n	a	s	a
Record Status	Type of record	Bibliographical level	Descriptive Catg.Form

CONTROL FIELD –MONOGRAPH & SERIAL (008)

t	2 0 0 5		n y u	a	f
Type of Date	Date1	Date2	Place of Publ.	Illustration	Target Audience

#					1	#	
Form Of Item	Nature of Contents	Govt. Pub.	Conf. Pub.	Festschrift	Index	Undefined	Literary Form

	e n g	#	
Biography	Language	Modified Record	Cata. Source

NAME OF THE FIELD INCL. MARC21 TAG	INDICATORS 1	2	DATA WITH SUBFIELD IDENTIFIERS
ISBN NO. (020) (R)	#	#	$a $c 400.00
ISSN (022) (R)	#	#	$a 0733-8724
DEWEY DECIMAL CLASSIFICATION NUMBER (082) (R)	0	#	$a 621.305 $b 20th ed
MAIN ENTRY-PERSONAL NAME (100) (NR)			$a $b $c
MAIN ENTRY – CORPORATE NAME (110) NR			$a $b $c $d $n
MAIN ENTRY – MEETING name (111) (NR)			$a $c $d $e $n
MAIN ENTRY - UNIFORM TITLE (130) (NR)			$a $d $k $l $n
KEY TITLE (222)	#		$a Journal of lightwave technology $b
TITLE STATEMENT (245) (NR)			$a
EDITION STATEMENT (250) (nr)	#	#	$a
PUBLICATION DIST.	3	#	$a New York

ETC.(260) ®			$b Institute of Electrical and Electronics Engineers (IEEE) $c 2005(May.)
PHYSICAL DESC. (300) ®	#	#	$a V.23,no.5 $b $c $e
SERIES STATEMENT/ ADDED ENTRY-TITLE (440) (R)	#		$a
SERIES STATEMENT (490)(R)			$a
GENERAL NOTE (500) (R)	#	#	$a Monthly
CONTENTS NOTE (505)(R)			$a
SUBJECT ADDED ENTRY- PERSONAL NAME (600) (R)			$a $b $c
SUBJECT ADDED ENTRY- CORPORATE NAME (610) (R)			$a $c $d
SUBJECT ADDED ENTRY- TOPICAL NAME (650) (R)	#	0	$a Lightwave technology $v Periodical $x $y $z
SUBJECT ADDED ENTRY- GEOGRAPHIC NAME (651) (R)			$a $v
ADDED ENTRY- PERSONAL NAME (700) (R)			$a $b $c
ADDED ENTRY-			$a

CORPORATE NAME (710) (R)			$b $c $d
ADDED ENTRY- MEETING NAME (711 (R)			$a $c $d
ADDED ENTRY – UNIFORM TITLE (730) (R)			$a
LOCATION (852)	1	#	$a
ACCESSION NO. INCL. DT. (901)			$a 5 $b 24.03.07 $c
CALL NO. (902)			$a 621.305P06
SUBJECT HEADING DEFINED BY (			$a S.Das
ENTERED BY (904)			$a S.Das
VERIFIED BY (905)			$a S.Das

NB. #= Put blank. R means Repeatable. NR means Not Repeatable

EXAMPLE 6

Library and Information Science Research: an International Journal

Elsevier

USA

December 2006

O.I.– Vol. 28, no. 2, May 2006 /

Subject: Library science / Quarterly journal /

ISSN: 0740-8188

MARC21: BIBLIOGRAPHIC FORMAT

LEADER (M):

n	a	s	a
Record Status	Type of record	Bibliographical level	Descriptive Catg.Form

CONTROL FIELD –MONOGRAPH & SERIAL (008)

t	2006		us#	a	f
Type of Date	Date1	Date2	Place of Publ.	Illustration	Target Audience

#					1	#	
Form Of Item	Nature of Contents	Govt. Pub.	Conf. Pub.	Festschrift	Index	Undefined	Literary Form

	eng	#	
Biography	Language	Modified Record	Cata. Source

NAME OF THE FIELD INCL. MARC21 TAG	INDICATORS 1	2	DATA WITH SUBFIELD IDENTIFIERS
ISBN NO. (020) (R)	#	#	$a $c 325.00
ISSN (022) (R)	#	#	$a 0740-8188
DEWEY DECIMAL CLASSIFICATION NUMBER (082) (R)	0	#	$a 020.5 $b 20th ed
MAIN ENTRY-PERSONAL NAME (100) (NR)			$a $b $c
MAIN ENTRY – CORPORATE NAME (110) NR			$a $b $c $d $n
MAIN ENTRY – MEETING name (111) (NR)			$a $c $d $e $n
MAIN ENTRY - UNIFORM TITLE (130) (NR)			$a $d $k $l $n
KEY TITLE(222)	#		$a Library and information science research: an international journal $b
TITLE STATEMENT (245) (NR)			$a
EDITION STATEMENT (250) (nr)	#	#	$a

PUBLICATION DIST. ETC.(260) ®	3	#	$a USA $b Elsevier $c 2006
PHYSICAL DESC. (300) ®	#	#	$a V.28,no.2 $b $c $e
SERIES STATEMENT/ ADDED ENTRY-TITLE (440) (R)	#		$a
SERIES STATEMENT (490)(R)			$a
GENERAL NOTE (500) (R)	#	#	$a Quarterly
CONTENTS NOTE (505)(R)			$a
SUBJECT ADDED ENTRY- PERSONAL NAME (600) (R)			$a $b $c
SUBJECT ADDED ENTRY- CORPORATE NAME (610) (R)			$a $c $d
SUBJECT ADDED ENTRY- TOPICAL NAME (650) (R)	#	0	$a Library science $v Periodical $x $y $z
SUBJECT ADDED ENTRY- GEOGRAPHIC NAME (651) (R)			$a $v
ADDED ENTRY- PERSONAL NAME (700) (R)			$a $b $c
ADDED ENTRY- CORPORATE NAME (710) (R)			$a $b $c $d

ADDED ENTRY- MEETING NAME (711 (R)			$a $c $d
ADDED ENTRY – UNIFORM TITLE (730) (R)			$a
LOCATION (852)	1	#	$a
ACCESSION NO. INCL. DT. (901)			$a 6 $b 10.06.07 $c
CALL NO. (902)			$a 020.5P06
SUBJECT HEADING DEFINED BY (903)			$a S.Das
ENTERED BY (904)			$a S.Das
VERIFIED BY (905)			$a S. Das

NB. #= Put blank. R means Repeatable. NR means Not Repeatable

EXAMPLE 7

Herald of Library Science

Lucknow Publishing House

Lucknow

January-April 2006

O.I.– Vol. 45, no. 1-2, January-April 2006 /
Subject: Library science/ Published monthly /
ISSN: 0018-0528

MARC21: BIBLIOGRAPHIC FORMAT

LEADER (M):

Record Status	Type of record	Bibliographical level	Descriptive Catg.Form
n	a	s	a

CONTROL FIELD –MONOGRAPH & SERIAL (008)

Type of Date	Date1	Date2	Place of Publ.	Illustration	Target Audience
t	2 0 0 6		l u i	a	f

Form Of Item	Nature of Contents	Govt. Pub.	Conf. Pub.	Festschrift	Index	Undefined	Literary Form
#					1	#	

Biography	Language	Modified Record	Cata. Source
	e n g	#	

NAME OF THE FIELD INCL. MARC21 TAG	INDICATORS 1	2	DATA WITH SUBFIELD IDENTIFIERS
ISBN NO. (020) (R)	#	#	$a $c 180.00
ISSN (022) (R)	#	#	$a 0018-0528
DEWEY DECIMAL CLASSIFICATION NUMBER (082) (R)	0	#	$a 020.5 $b 20th ed
MAIN ENTRY-PERSONAL NAME (100) (NR)			$a $b $c
MAIN ENTRY – CORPORATE NAME (110) NR			$a $b $c $d $n
MAIN ENTRY – MEETING name (111) (NR)			$a $c $d $e $n
MAIN ENTRY - UNIFORM TITLE (130) (NR)			$a $d $k $l $n
KEY TITLE(222)	#		$a Herald of library science $b
TITLE STATEMENT (245) (NR)			$a
EDITION STATEMENT (250) (nr)	#	#	$a
PUBLICATION DIST. ETC.(260) ®	3	#	$a Lucknow $b Lucknow Pub House

			$c 2006(Jan.-Apr.)
PHYSICAL DESC. (300) ®	#	#	$a V.45,no.1-2 $b $c $e
SERIES STATEMENT/ ADDED ENTRY-TITLE (440) (R)	#		$a
SERIES STATEMENT (490)(R)			$a
GENERAL NOTE (500) (R)	#	#	$a Monthly
CONTENTS NOTE (505)(R)			$a
SUBJECT ADDED ENTRY-PERSONAL NAME (600) (R)			$a $b $c
SUBJECT ADDED ENTRY- CORPORATE NAME (610) (R)			$a $c $d
SUBJECT ADDED ENTRY- TOPICAL NAME (650) (R)	#	0	$a Library science $v Periodical $x $y $z
SUBJECT ADDED ENTRY-GEOGRAPHIC NAME (651) (R)			$a $v
ADDED ENTRY- PERSONAL NAME (700) (R)			$a $b $c
ADDED ENTRY-CORPORATE NAME (710) (R)			$a $b $c $d
ADDED ENTRY-MEETING NAME			$a $c

(711 (R)			$d
ADDED ENTRY – UNIFORM TITLE (730) (R)			$a
LOCATION (852)	1	#	$a
ACCESSION NO. INCL. DT. (901)			$a 7 $b 10.06.07 $c
CALL NO. (902)			$a 020.5P06
SUBJECT HEADING DEFINED BY (903)			$a S.Das
ENTERED BY (904)			$a S.Das
VERIFIED BY (905)			$a S.Das

NB. #= Put blank. R means Repeatable. NR means Not Repeatable

EXAMPLE 8

Annals of Library and Information Studies

Indian National Scientific Documentation Centre

New Delhi

June 2002

O.I.– Vol. 49, no. 2, June 2002/

Subject: Library science /Published quarterly /

ISSN: 0972-5423

MARC21: BIBLIOGRAPHIC FORMAT

LEADER (M):

Record Status	Type of record	Bibliographical level	Descriptive Catg.Form
n	a	s	a

CONTROL FIELD –MONOGRAPH & SERIAL (008)

Type of Date	Date1	Date2	Place of Publ.	Illustration	Target Audience
t	2 0 0 2		n d i	a	f

Form Of Item	Nature of Contents	Govt. Pub.	Conf. Pub.	Festschrift	Index	Undefined	Literary Form
#					1	#	

Biography	Language	Modified Record	Cata. Source
	e n g	#	

NAME OF THE FIELD INCL. MARC21 TAG	INDICATORS 1	2	DATA WITH SUBFIELD IDENTIFIERS
ISBN NO. (020) (R)	#	#	$a $c 150.00
ISSN (022) (R)	#	#	$a 0972-5423
DEWEY DECIMAL CLASSIFICATION NUMBER (082) (R)	0	#	$a 020.5 $b 20th ed
MAIN ENTRY-PERSONAL NAME (100) (NR)			$a $b $c
MAIN ENTRY – CORPORATE NAME (110) NR			$a $b $c $d $n
MAIN ENTRY – MEETING name (111) (NR)			$a $c $d $e $n
MAIN ENTRY - UNIFORM TITLE (130) (NR)			$a $d $k $l $n
KEY TITLE(222)	#		$a Annals of library and information studies $b
TITLE STATEMENT (245) (NR)			$a
EDITION STATEMENT (250) (nr)	#	#	$a
PUBLICATION DIST.	3	#	$a New Delhi

ETC.(260) ®			$b Indian National Scientific Documentation Centre $c 2002 (June.)
PHYSICAL DESC. (300) ®	#	#	$a V.49,no.2 $b $c $e
SERIES STATEMENT/ ADDED ENTRY-TITLE (440) (R)	#		$a
SERIES STATEMENT (490)(R)			$a
GENERAL NOTE (500) (R)	#	#	$a Quarterly
CONTENTS NOTE (505)(R)			$a
SUBJECT ADDED ENTRY- PERSONAL NAME (600) (R)			$a $b $c
SUBJECT ADDED ENTRY- CORPORATE NAME (610) (R)			$a $c $d
SUBJECT ADDED ENTRY- TOPICAL NAME (650) (R)	#	0	$a Library science $v Periodical $x $y $z
SUBJECT ADDED ENTRY- GEOGRAPHIC NAME (651) (R)			$a $v
ADDED ENTRY- PERSONAL NAME (700) (R)			$a $b $c
ADDED ENTRY- CORPORATE NAME			$a $b

(710) (R)			$c $d
ADDED ENTRY- MEETING NAME (711 (R)			$a $c $d
ADDED ENTRY – UNIFORM TITLE (730) (R)			$a
LOCATION (852)	1	#	$a
ACCESSION NO. INCL. DT. (901)			$a 8 $b 10.06.07 $c
CALL NO. (902)			$a 020.5P02
SUBJECT HEADING DEFINED BY (903)			$a S.Das
ENTERED BY (904)			$a S.Das
VERIFIED BY (905)			$a S.Das

NB. #= Put blank. R means Repeatable. NR means Not Repeatable

EXAMPLE 9

Journal of Documentation

Emerald

UK

April 2005

O.I.– Vol. 61, no. 4, April 2005 /
Subject: Library science / Monthly published /
ISSN: 0022-0418

MARC21: BIBLIOGRAPHIC FORMAT

LEADER (M):

Record Status	Type of record	Bibliographical level	Descriptive Catg.Form
n	a	s	a

CONTROL FIELD –MONOGRAPH & SERIAL (008)

Type of Date	Date1	Date2	Place of Publ.	Illustration	Target Audience
t	2 0 0 5		u k #	a	f

Form Of Item	Nature of Contents	Govt. Pub.	Conf. Pub.	Festschrift	Index	Undefined	Literary Form
#					1	#	

Biography	Language	Modified Record	Cata. Source
	eng	#	

NAME OF THE FIELD INCL. MARC21 TAG	INDICATORS 1	2	DATA WITH SUBFIELD IDENTIFIERS
ISBN NO. (020) (R)	#	#	$a $c 200.00
ISSN (022) (R)	#	#	$a 0022-0418
DEWEY DECIMAL CLASSIFICATION NUMBER (082) (R)	0	#	$a 020.5 $b 20th ed
MAIN ENTRY-PERSONAL NAME (100) (NR)			$a $b $c
MAIN ENTRY – CORPORATE NAME (110) NR			$a $b $c $d $n
MAIN ENTRY – MEETING name (111) (NR)			$a $c $d $e $n
MAIN ENTRY - UNIFORM TITLE (130) (NR)			$a $d $k $l $n
KEY TITLE(222)	#		$a Journal of documentation $b
TITLE STATEMENT (245) (NR)			$a
EDITION STATEMENT (250) (nr)	#	#	$a
PUBLICATION DIST.	3	#	$a UK

ETC.(260) ®			$b Emerald $c 2005
PHYSICAL DESC. (300) ®	#	#	$a V.61,no.4 $b $c $e
SERIES STATEMENT/ ADDED ENTRY-TITLE (440) (R)	#		$a
SERIES STATEMENT (490)(R)			$a
GENERAL NOTE (500) (R)	#	#	$a Monthly
CONTENTS NOTE (505)(R)			$a
SUBJECT ADDED ENTRY- PERSONAL NAME (600) (R)			$a $b $c
SUBJECT ADDED ENTRY- CORPORATE NAME (610) (R)			$a $c $d
SUBJECT ADDED ENTRY- TOPICAL NAME (650) (R)	#	0	$a Library science $v Periodical $x $y $z
SUBJECT ADDED ENTRY- GEOGRAPHIC NAME (651) (R)			$a $v
ADDED ENTRY- PERSONAL NAME (700) (R)			$a $b $c
ADDED ENTRY- CORPORATE NAME (710) (R)			$a $b $c

			$d
ADDED ENTRY- MEETING NAME (711 (R)			$a $c $d
ADDED ENTRY – UNIFORM TITLE (730) (R)			$a
LOCATION (852)	1	#	$a
ACCESSION NO. INCL. DT. (901)			$a 9 $b 10.06.07 $c
CALL NO. (902)			$a 020.5P05
SUBJECT HEADING DEFINED BY (903)			$a S.Das
ENTERED BY (904)			$a S.Das
VERIFIED BY (905)			$a S.Das

NB. #= Put blank. R means Repeatable. NR means Not Repeatable

EXAMPLE 10

Library Resources and Technical Services

American Library Association
Chicago
October 2004

O.I.– Vol. 48, no. 4, October 2003/
Subject: Library science /Quarterly published /
ISSN: 0024-2527

MARC21: BIBLIOGRAPHIC FORMAT

LEADER (M):

Record Status	Type of record	Bibliographical level	Descriptive Catg.Form
n	a	s	a

CONTROL FIELD –MONOGRAPH & SERIAL (008)

Type of Date	Date1	Date2	Place of Publ.	Illustration	Target Audience
t	2 0 0 4		c h u	a	f

Form Of Item	Nature of Contents	Govt. Pub.	Conf. Pub.	Festschrift	Index	Undefined	Literary Form
#					1	#	

Biography	Language	Modified Record	Cata. Source
	e n g	#	

NAME OF THE FIELD INCL. MARC21 TAG	INDICATORS 1	2	DATA WITH SUBFIELD IDENTIFIERS
ISBN NO. (020) (R)	#	#	$a $c 125.00
ISSN (022) (R)	#	#	$a 0024-2527
DEWEY DECIMAL CLASSIFICATION NUMBER (082) (R)	0	#	$a 020.5 $b 20th ed
MAIN ENTRY-PERSONAL NAME (100) (NR)			$a $b $c
MAIN ENTRY – CORPORATE NAME (110) NR			$a $b $c $d $n
MAIN ENTRY – MEETING name (111) (NR)			$a $c $d $e $n
MAIN ENTRY - UNIFORM TITLE (130) (NR)			$a $d $k $l $n
KEY TITLE(222)	#		$a Library resources and technical services $b
TITLE STATEMENT (245) (NR)			$a
EDITION STATEMENT (250) (nr)	#	#	$a
PUBLICATION DIST.	3	#	$a Chicago

ETC.(260) ®			$b American Library Association $c 2004(Oct.)
PHYSICAL DESC. (300) ®	#	#	$a V.48,no.4 $b $c $e
SERIES STATEMENT/ ADDED ENTRY-TITLE (440) (R)	#		$a
SERIES STATEMENT (490)(R)			$a
GENERAL NOTE (500) (R)	#	#	$a Quarterly
CONTENTS NOTE (505)(R)			$a
SUBJECT ADDED ENTRY- PERSONAL NAME (600) (R)			$a $b $c
SUBJECT ADDED ENTRY- CORPORATE NAME (610) (R)			$a $c $d
SUBJECT ADDED ENTRY- TOPICAL NAME (650) (R)	#	0	$a Library science $v Periodical $x $y $z
SUBJECT ADDED ENTRY- GEOGRAPHIC NAME (651) (R)			$a $v
ADDED ENTRY- PERSONAL NAME (700) (R)			$a $b $c
ADDED ENTRY- CORPORATE NAME			$a $b

(710) (R)			$c $d
ADDED ENTRY- MEETING NAME (711 (R)			$a $c $d
ADDED ENTRY – UNIFORM TITLE (730) (R)			$a
LOCATION (852)	1	#	$a
ACCESSION NO. INCL. DT. (901)			$a 10 $b 10.06.07 $c
CALL NO. (902)			$a 020.5P09
SUBJECT HEADING DEFINED BY (903)			$a S.Das
ENTERED BY (904)			$a S.Das
VERIFIED BY (905)			$a S.Das

NB. #= Put blank. R means Repeatable. NR means Not Repeatable

4

MARC 21: Bibliographic Format of Composite Books

EXAMPLE 11

BLACKWELL'S FRENCH TEXTS

General Editor: Alfred Ewerd

VOLTAIRE

Letters philosophiques

Edited by
F. A. TAYLOR

Œ

Basil Blackwell
Oxford
1965

O.I.: Pages – 122 / Size - 23 cm / Contains - Two sisters, by R.L. Stevenson. P. 1-20

MARC21: BIBLIOGRAPHIC FORMAT

LEADER (M):

n	a	m	a
Record Status	Type of record	Bibliographical level	Descriptive Catg.Form

CONTROL FIELD-MONOGRAPH & SERIAL (008)

t	1 9 6 5		o x n	a	g
Type of Date	Date1	Date2	Place of Publ.	Illustration	Target Audience

#						#	
Form Of Item	Nature of Contents	Govt. Pub.	Conf. Pub.	Festschrift	Index	Undefined	Literary Form

	e n g	#	
Biography	Language	Modified Record	Cata. Source

NAME OF THE FIELD INCL. MARC21 TAG	INDICATORS 1	2	DATA WITH SUBFIELD IDENTIFIERS
ISBN NO. (020) (R)	#	#	$a 012738512-X $c
ISSN (022) (R)	#	#	$a
DEWEY DECIMAL CLASSIFICATION NUMBER (082) (R)	0	#	$a 824.0254 $b 20th ed
MAIN ENTRY-PERSONAL NAME (100) (NR)			$a Ewerd, Alfred $b $c
MAIN ENTRY –CORPORATE NAME (110) (NR)		#	$a $b $c $d $n
MAIN ENTRY – MEETING NAME (111) (NR)		#	$a $c $d $e $n
MAIN ENTRY - UNIFORM TITLE (130) (NR)		#	$a $d $k $l $n
KEY TITLE(222)			$a $b
TITLA STATEMENT (245) (NR)			$a Blackwell French texts $b $c
EDITION STATEMENT (250) (nr)	#	#	$a 2nd ed $b

PUBLICATION DIST. ETC.(260) ®	3	#	$a Oxford $b Basil Blackwell $c 1965
PHYSICAL DESC. (300) ®	#	#	$a 122p. $b Ill. $c 23 cm. $e
SERIES STATEMENT/ ADDED ENTRY-TITLE (440) (R)	#		$a $n
SERIES STATEMENT (490)(R)		#	$a
GENERAL NOTE (500) (R)	#	#	$a Includes index. – This is the collection of English essays
CONTENTS NOTE (505) (R)		#	$a Two sisters/ by R.L. Stevenson p.1 - 20
SUBJECT ADDED ENTRY- PERSONAL NAME (600) (R)		0	$a $b $c
SUBJECT ADDED ENTRY- CORPORATE NAME (610) (R)		0	$a $c $d
SUBJECT ADDED ENTRY- TOPICAL NAME (650) (R)		0	$a English essays $v $x $y $z
SUBJECT ADDED ENTRY- GEOGRAPHIC NAME (651) (R)	#	0	$a $v
ADDED ENTRY- PERSONAL NAME (700) (R)		#	$a Stevenson, R.L., Taylor, F.A., ed. $b $c

ADDED ENTRY- CORPORATE NAME (710) (R)		#	$a $b $c $d
ADDED ENTRY- MEETING NAME (711 (R)		#	$a $c $d
ADDED ENTRY – UNIFORM TITLE (730) (R)		#	$a
LOCATION (852)	1	#	$a
ACCESSION NO. INCL. DT. (901)			$a 11 $b 10-06-07 $c
CALL NO. (902)			$a 824.0254K65
SUBJECT HEADING DEFINED BY (903)			$a S.Das
ENTERED BY (904)			$a S.Das
VERIFIED BY (905)			$a S.Das

NB. #= Put blank. R means Repeatable. NR means Not Repeatable

EXAMPLE 12

Collections of funny stories

For children

Editor:

SALLEY E. MOON

VACATION WORK

Pearl End Street

Oxford

1956

O.I.: Pages - 217 / Size - 22 cm / Contains - Bleak Morning, by John Glsworthy. P. 22-42

MARC21: BIBLIOGRAPHIC FORMAT

LEADER (M):

Record Status	Type of record	Bibliographical level	Descriptive Catg.Form
n	a	m	a

CONTROL FIELD-MONOGRAPH & SERIAL (008)

Type of Date	Date1	Date2	Place of Publ.	Illustration	Target Audience
t	1 9 5 6		o x n	a	g

Form Of Item	Nature of Contents	Govt. Pub.	Conf. Pub.	Festschrift	Index	Undefined	Literary Form
#						#	

Biography	Language	Modified Record	Cata. Source
	e n g	#	

NAME OF THE FIELD INCL. MARC21 TAG	INDICATORS 1	2	DATA WITH SUBFIELD IDENTIFIERS
ISBN NO. (020) (R)	#	#	$a 012738512-X $c
ISSN (022) (R)	#	#	$a
DEWEY DECIMAL CLASSIFICATION NUMBER (082) (R)	0	#	$a 823.0224 $b 20th ed
MAIN ENTRY-PERSONAL NAME (100) (NR)			$a $b $c
MAIN ENTRY – CORPORATE NAME (110) (NR)		#	$a $b $c $d $n
MAIN ENTRY – MEETING NAME (111) (NR)		#	$a $c $d $e $n
MAIN ENTRY - UNIFORM TITLE (130) (NR)		#	$a $d $k $l $n
KEY TITLE(222)			$a $b
TITLA STATEMENT (245) (NR)			$a Collection of funny stories for children $b $c
EDITION STATEMENT (250) (nr)	#	#	$a 2nd ed $b

PUBLICATION DIST. ETC.(260) ®	3	#	$a Oxford $b Vacation Work $c 1956
PHYSICAL DESC. (300) ®	#	#	$a 217p. $b ill. $c 22 cm. $e
SERIES STATEMENT/ ADDED ENTRY-TITLE (440) (R)	#		$a $n
SERIES STATEMENT (490)(R)		#	$a
GENERAL NOTE (500) (R)	#	#	$a Includes index. – This is the collection of English essays
CONTENTS NOTE (505) (R)		#	$a Bleak Morning/ by John Glsworthy. P. 22 - 42
SUBJECT ADDED ENTRY- PERSONAL NAME (600) (R)		0	$a $b $c
SUBJECT ADDED ENTRY- CORPORATE NAME (610) (R)		0	$a $c $d
SUBJECT ADDED ENTRY- TOPICAL NAME (650) (R)		0	$a English essays $v $x $y $z
SUBJECT ADDED ENTRY- GEOGRAPHIC NAME (651) (R)	#	0	$a $v
ADDED ENTRY- PERSONAL NAME (700) (R)		#	$a John, Glsworthy, Salleye, Moon E., <u>ed.</u> $b $c

ADDED ENTRY- CORPORATE NAME (710) (R)		#	$a $b $c $d
ADDED ENTRY- MEETING NAME (711 (R)		#	$a $c $d
ADDED ENTRY – UNIFORM TITLE (730) (R)		#	$a
LOCATION (852)	1	#	$a
ACCESSION NO. INCL. DT. (901)			$a 12 $b 10-06-07 $c
CALL NO. (902)			$a 823.0224J56
SUBJECT HEADING DEFINED BY (903)			$a S.Das
ENTERED BY (904)			$a S.Das
VERIFIED BY (905)			$a S.Das

NB. #= Put blank. R means Repeatable. NR means Not Repeatable

EXAMPLE 13

Modern Studies in Philosophy Descartes
A collection of critical essays

EDITED BY

WILLS DONEY

MACMILLAN

London, Melbourne

1968

O.I.: Pages - 89 / Size - 23 cm / Contains - The Hotel, by George Meredith p. 22-42

MARC21: BIBLIOGRAPHIC FORMAT

LEADER (M):

n	a	m	a
Record Status	Type of record	Bibliographical level	Descriptive Catg.Form

CONTROL FIELD-MONOGRAPH & SERIAL (008)

t	1 9 6 8		l o #	a	g
Type of Date	Date1	Date2	Place of Publ.	Illustration	Target Audience

#						#	
Form Of Item	Nature of Contents	Govt. Pub.	Conf. Pub.	Festschrift	Index	Undefined	Literary Form

	e n g	#	
Biography	Language	Modified Record	Cata. Source

NAME OF THE FIELD INCL. MARC21 TAG	INDICATORS 1	2	DATA WITH SUBFIELD IDENTIFIERS
ISBN NO. (020) (R)	#	#	$a 012738512-X $c
ISSN (022) (R)	#	#	$a
DEWEY DECIMAL CLASSIFICATION NUMBER (082) (R)	0	#	$a 821.521 $b 20th ed
MAIN ENTRY-PERSONAL NAME (100) (NR)			$a $b $c
MAIN ENTRY – CORPORATE NAME (110) (NR)		#	$a $b $c $d $n
MAIN ENTRY – MEETING NAME (111) (NR)		#	$a $c $d $e $n
MAIN ENTRY - UNIFORM TITLE (130) (NR)		#	$a $d $k $l $n
KEY TITLE(222)			$a $b
TITLA STATEMENT (245) (NR)			$a Collection of critical essays $b $c
EDITION STATEMENT (250) (nr)	#	#	$a 2nd ed $b

PUBLICATION DIST. ETC.(260) ®	3	#	$a London $b Macmillan $c 1968
PHYSICAL DESC. (300) ®	#	#	$a 89p. $b ill. $c 23 cm. $e
SERIES STATEMENT/ ADDED ENTRY-TITLE (440) (R)	#		$a $n
SERIES STATEMENT (490)(R)		#	$a
GENERAL NOTE (500) (R)	#	#	$a This is the collection of English essays
CONTENTS NOTE (505) (R)		#	$a The Hotel/ by George Meredith p. 22-42
SUBJECT ADDED ENTRY- PERSONAL NAME (600) (R)		0	$a $b $c
SUBJECT ADDED ENTRY- CORPORATE NAME (610) (R)		0	$a $c $d
SUBJECT ADDED ENTRY- TOPICAL NAME (650) (R)		0	$a $v $x $y $z
SUBJECT ADDED ENTRY- GEOGRAPHIC NAME (651) (R)	#	0	$a $v
ADDED ENTRY- PERSONAL NAME (700) (R)		#	$a Meredith, George, Doney, Wills, ed. $b $c
ADDED ENTRY-		#	$a

CORPORATE NAME (710) (R)			$b $c $d
ADDED ENTRY- MEETING NAME (711 (R)		#	$a $c $d
ADDED ENTRY – UNIFORM TITLE (730) (R)		#	$a
LOCATION (852)	1	#	$a
ACCESSION NO. INCL. DT. (901)			$a 13 $b 10-06-07 $c
CALL NO. (902)			$a 821.521K68
SUBJECT HEADING DEFINED BY (903)			$a S.Das
ENTERED BY (904)			$a S.Das
VERIFIED BY (905)			$a S.Das

NB. #= Put blank. R means Repeatable. NR means Not Repeatable

EXAMPLE 14

World Best Hunting Stories
Collections of English Stories

Compiled by:
WILLIAM PETGER WOALKER

Frederick Warne Ltd
London
1992

O.I.: Pages - 215 / Size - 23 cm. / ISBN: 012-738512-X /

Contains - The Lion and his cave, by W. P. Sengondge.
P. 12-28

MARC21: BIBLIOGRAPHIC FORMAT

LEADER (M):

Record Status	Type of record	Bibliographical level	Descriptive Catg.Form
n	a	m	a

CONTROL FIELD-MONOGRAPH & SERIAL (008)

Type of Date	Date1	Date2	Place of Publ.	Illustration	Target Audience
t	1 9 9 2		l o #	a	g

Form Of Item	Nature of Contents	Govt. Pub.	Conf. Pub.	Festschrift	Index	Undefined	Literary Form
#						#	

Biography	Language	Modified Record	Cata. Source
	e n g	#	

NAME OF THE FIELD INCL. MARC21 TAG	INDICATORS 1	2	DATA WITH SUBFIELD IDENTIFIERS
ISBN NO. (020) (R)	#	#	$a 012738512-X $c
ISSN (022) (R)	#	#	$a
DEWEY DECIMAL CLASSIFICATION NUMBER (082) (R)	0	#	$a 823.10254 $b 20th ed
MAIN ENTRY-PERSONAL NAME (100) (NR)			$a $b $c
MAIN ENTRY – CORPORATE NAME (110) (NR)		#	$a $b $c $d $n
MAIN ENTRY – MEETING NAME (111) (NR)		#	$a $c $d $e $n
MAIN ENTRY - UNIFORM TITLE (130) (NR)		#	$a $d $k $l $n
KEY TITLE(222)			$a $b
TITLA STATEMENT (245) (NR)			$a World best hunting stories $b Collection of English stories $c
EDITION STATEMENT (250) (nr)	#	#	$a 2nd ed $b

PUBLICATION DIST. ETC.(260) ®	3	#	$a London $b Frederick Warne $c 1992
PHYSICAL DESC. (300) ®	#	#	$a 215p. $b ill. $c 23 cm. $e
SERIES STATEMENT/ ADDED ENTRY-TITLE (440) (R)	#		$a $n
SERIES STATEMENT (490)(R)		#	$a
GENERAL NOTE (500) (R)	#	#	$a This is the collection of English essays
CONTENTS NOTE (505) (R)		#	$a The Lion and his cave, by W. P. Sengondge. p. 12-28
SUBJECT ADDED ENTRY- PERSONAL NAME (600) (R)		0	$a $b $c
SUBJECT ADDED ENTRY- CORPORATE NAME (610) (R)		0	$a $c $d
SUBJECT ADDED ENTRY-TOPICAL NAME (650) (R)		0	$a English essays $v $x $y $z
SUBJECT ADDED ENTRY-GEOGRAPHIC NAME (651) (R)	#	0	$a $v
ADDED ENTRY-PERSONAL NAME (700) (R)		#	$a Sengondge, W.P., Woalker, William Petger, comp. $b $c

ADDED ENTRY- CORPORATE NAME (710) (R)		#	$a $b $c $d
ADDED ENTRY- MEETING NAME (711 (R)		#	$a $c $d
ADDED ENTRY – UNIFORM TITLE (730) (R)		#	$a
LOCATION (852)	1	#	$a
ACCESSION NO. INCL. DT. (901)			$a 14 $b 10-06-07 $c
CALL NO. (902)			$a 823.10254N92
SUBJECT HEADING DEFINED BY (903)			$a S.Das
ENTERED BY (904)			$a S.Das
VERIFIED BY (905)			$a S.Das

NB. #= Put blank. R means Repeatable. NR means Not Repeatable

EXAMPLE 15

The Observer's Books of Wild Animals Of the British Isles

Compiled by:

W. J. STROKE

Maurice Burton

London

1965

O.I.: Pages - 125 / Size - 22 cm /Contains - The snake and the tiger's roar, by W. G. Gallstone P. 51-75

MARC21: BIBLIOGRAPHIC FORMAT

LEADER (M):

n	a	m	a
Record Status	Type of record	Bibliographical level	Descriptive Catg.Form

CONTROL FIELD-MONOGRAPH & SERIAL (008)

t	1 9 6 5		l o #	a	g
Type of Date	Date1	Date2	Place of Publ.	Illustration	Target Audience

#						#	
Form Of Item	Nature of Contents	Govt. Pub.	Conf. Pub.	Festschrift	Index	Undefined	Literary Form

	e n g	#	
Biography	Language	Modified Record	Cata. Source

NAME OF THE FIELD INCL. MARC21 TAG	INDICATORS 1	2	DATA WITH SUBFIELD IDENTIFIERS
ISBN NO. (020) (R)	#	#	$a 012738512-X $c
ISSN (022) (R)	#	#	$a
DEWEY DECIMAL CLASSIFICATION NUMBER (082) (R)	0	#	$a 820.419 $b 20th ed
MAIN ENTRY-PERSONAL NAME (100) (NR)			$a $b $c
MAIN ENTRY –CORPORATE NAME (110) (NR)		#	$a $b $c $d $n
MAIN ENTRY – MEETING NAME (111) (NR)		#	$a $c $d $e $n
MAIN ENTRY - UNIFORM TITLE (130) (NR)		#	$a $d $k $l $n
KEY TITLE(222)			$a $b
TITLA STATEMENT (245) (NR)			$a The observer's book of world animals $b Of the British Isles $c
EDITION STATEMENT (250) (nr)	#	#	$a 2nd ed $b

PUBLICATION DIST. ETC.(260) ®	3	#	$a London $b Maurice Burton $c 1965
PHYSICAL DESC. (300) ®	#	#	$a 125p. $b ill. $c 22 cm. $e
SERIES STATEMENT/ ADDED ENTRY-TITLE (440) (R)	#		$a $n
SERIES STATEMENT (490)(R)		#	$a
GENERAL NOTE (500) (R)	#	#	$a Includes index. – This is the collection of the English essays
CONTENTS NOTE (505) (R)		#	$a The snake and the tiger's roar/ by W. G. Gallstone p. 51-75
SUBJECT ADDED ENTRY- PERSONAL NAME (600) (R)		0	$a $b $c
SUBJECT ADDED ENTRY- CORPORATE NAME (610) (R		0	$a $c $d
SUBJECT ADDED ENTRY- TOPICAL NAME (650) (R)		0	$a English essays $v $x $y $z
SUBJECT ADDED ENTRY- GEOGRAPHIC NAME (651) (R)	#	0	$a $v
ADDED ENTRY- PERSONAL NAME (700) (R)		#	$a Glasstone, W.G., Stroke, W.J., comp. $b $c

ADDED ENTRY- CORPORATE NAME (710) (R)		#	$a $b $c $d
ADDED ENTRY- MEETING NAME (711 (R)		#	$a $c $d
ADDED ENTRY – UNIFORM TITLE (730) (R)		#	$a
LOCATION (852)	1	#	$a
ACCESSION NO. INCL. DT. (901)			$a 15 $b 10-06-07 $c
CALL NO. (902)			$a 820.419K65
SUBJECT HEADING DEFINED BY (903)			$a S.Das
ENTERED BY (904)			$a S.Das
VERIFIED BY (905)			$a S.Das

NB. #= Put blank. R means Repeatable. NR means Not Repeatable

EXAMPLE 16

Collected Essays

Edited by

F. A. Greene

Bodley Head

London

1969

O.I.: Pages - 122 / Size - 24 cm. / Colour illustration /
Contains - claver lad, by Bunting Basil P. 1-20

MARC21: BIBLIOGRAPHIC FORMAT

LEADER (M):

n	a	m	a
Record Status	Type of record	Bibliographical level	Descriptive Catg.Form

CONTROL FIELD-MONOGRAPH & SERIAL (008)

t	1 9 6 9		l o #	a	g
Type of Date	Date1	Date2	Place of Publ.	Illustration	Target Audience

#						#	
Form Of Item	Nature of Contents	Govt. Pub.	Conf. Pub.	Festschrift	Index	Undefined	Literary Form

	e n g	#	
Biography	Language	Modified Record	Cata. Source

NAME OF THE FIELD INCL. MARC21 TAG	INDICATORS 1	2	DATA WITH SUBFIELD IDENTIFIERS
ISBN NO. (020) (R)	#	#	$a 012738512-X $c
ISSN (022) (R)	#	#	$a
DEWEY DECIMAL CLASSIFICATION NUMBER (082) (R)	0	#	$a 824.0254 $b 20th ed
MAIN ENTRY-PERSONAL NAME (100) (NR)			$a $b $c
MAIN ENTRY – CORPORATE NAME (110) (NR)		#	$a $b $c $d $n
MAIN ENTRY – MEETING NAME (111) (NR)		#	$a $c $d $e $n
MAIN ENTRY - UNIFORM TITLE (130) (NR)		#	$a $d $k $l $n
KEY TITLE(222)			$a $b
TITLA STATEMENT (245) (NR)			$a Collected essays $b $c
EDITION STATEMENT (250) (nr)	#	#	$a 2nd ed $b
PUBLICATION DIST.	3	#	$a London

ETC.(260) ®			$b Bodley Head $c 1969
PHYSICAL DESC. (300) ®	#	#	$a 463p. $b ill. $c 24 cm. $e
SERIES STATEMENT/ ADDED ENTRY-TITLE (440) (R)	#		$a $n
SERIES STATEMENT (490)(R)		#	$a
GENERAL NOTE (500) (R)	#	#	$a Includes index. – This is the collection of the English essays
CONTENTS NOTE (505) (R)		#	$a Claver lad/ by Bunting Basil p. 1-20
SUBJECT ADDED ENTRY- PERSONAL NAME (600) (R)		0	$a $b $c
SUBJECT ADDED ENTRY- CORPORATE NAME (610) (R)		0	$a $c $d
SUBJECT ADDED ENTRY- TOPICAL NAME (650) (R)		0	$a English essays $v $x $y $z
SUBJECT ADDED ENTRY- GEOGRAPHIC NAME (651) (R)	#	0	$a $v
ADDED ENTRY- PERSONAL NAME (700) (R)		#	$a Basil, Bunting, Green, G., ed. $b $c
ADDED ENTRY-		#	$a

CORPORATE NAME (710) (R)			$b $c $d
ADDED ENTRY- MEETING NAME (711 (R)		#	$a $c $d
ADDED ENTRY – UNIFORM TITLE (730) (R)		#	$a
LOCATION (852)	1	#	$a
ACCESSION NO. INCL. DT. (901)			$a 16 $b 10-06-07 $c
CALL NO. (902)			$a 824.0254K69
SUBJECT HEADING DEFINED BY (903)			$a S.Das
ENTERED BY (904)			$a S.Das
VERIFIED BY (905)			$a S.Das

NB. #= Put blank. R means Repeatable. NR means Not Repeatable

EXAMPLE 17

Collected Short Stories

Edited by

WILLETT, RALF

Minarva

London

1965

O.I.: ISBN: 012-858517-X / Pages - 345 / Size - 23 cm. /
Contains - Hunting tiger, by Soyinka, Wole. P. 35-37

MARC21: BIBLIOGRAPHIC FORMAT

LEADER (M):

Record Status	Type of record	Bibliographical level	Descriptive Catg.Form
n	a	m	a

CONTROL FIELD-MONOGRAPH & SERIAL (008)

Type of Date	Date1	Date2	Place of Publ.	Illustration	Target Audience
t	1 9 9 2		l o #	a	g

Form Of Item	Nature of Contents	Govt. Pub.	Conf. Pub.	Festschrift	Index	Undefined	Literary Form
#						#	

Biography	Language	Modified Record	Cata. Source
	e n g	#	

NAME OF THE FIELD INCL. MARC21 TAG	INDICATORS 1	2	DATA WITH SUBFIELD IDENTIFIERS
ISBN NO. (020) (R)	#	#	$a 012858517-X $c
ISSN (022) (R)	#	#	$a
DEWEY DECIMAL CLASSIFICATION NUMBER (082) (R)	0	#	$a 820.73231 $b 20th ed
MAIN ENTRY-PERSONAL NAME (100) (NR)			$a $b $c
MAIN ENTRY – CORPORATE NAME (110) (NR)		#	$a $b $c $d $n
MAIN ENTRY – MEETING NAME (111) (NR)		#	$a $c $d $e $n
MAIN ENTRY - UNIFORM TITLE (130) (NR)		#	$a $d $k $l $n
KEY TITLE(222)			$a $b
TITLA STATEMENT (245) (NR)			$a Collected short stories $b $c
EDITION STATEMENT (250) (nr)	#	#	$a 2nd ed $b

PUBLICATION DIST. ETC.(260) ®	3	#	$a London $b Minerva $c 1992
PHYSICAL DESC. (300) ®	#	#	$a 345p. $b $c 23cm. $e
SERIES STATEMENT/ ADDED ENTRY-TITLE (440) (R)	#		$a $n
SERIES STATEMENT (490)(R)		#	$a
GENERAL NOTE (500) (R)	#	#	$a Includes illustration. – This is the collection of English short stories for children
CONTENTS NOTE (505) (R)		#	$a Hunting tiger/ by Soyinka, Wole. p. 35-37
SUBJECT ADDED ENTRY-PERSONAL NAME (600) (R)		0	$a $b $c
SUBJECT ADDED ENTRY-CORPORATE NAME (610) (R)		0	$a $c $d
SUBJECT ADDED ENTRY-TOPICAL NAME (650) (R)		0	$a English short stories $v $x $y $z
SUBJECT ADDED ENTRY-GEOGRAPHIC NAME (651) (R)	#	0	$a $v
ADDED ENTRY- PERSONAL NAME (700) (R)		#	$a Wole, Soyinka, Willett, Ralf, ed. $b

			$c
ADDED ENTRY- CORPORATE NAME (710) (R)		#	$a $b $c $d
ADDED ENTRY- MEETING NAME (711) (R)		#	$a $c $d
ADDED ENTRY – UNIFORM TITLE (730) (R)		#	$a
LOCATION (852)	1	#	$a
ACCESSION NO. INCL. DT. (901)			$a 17 $b 10-06-07 $c
CALL NO. (902)			$a 820.73231N92
SUBJECT HEADING DEFINED BY (903)			$a S.Das
ENTERED BY (904)			$a S.Das
VERIFIED BY (905)			$a S.Das

NB. #= Put blank. R means Repeatable. NR means Not Repeatable

EXAMPLE 18

Collected Fictions

General Editor: LUIS JORGE BORGES

Second Edition

Penguin Books

London

1998

O.I.: ISBN: 087-8457162-X / Pages - 565 / Size - 22 cm. / Contains - The Moon and the Sun, by Anderi Tarkovsky. P. 11-25

MARC21: BIBLIOGRAPHIC FORMAT

LEADER (M):

n	a	m	a
Record Status	Type of record	Bibliographical level	Descriptive Catg.Form

CONTROL FIELD-MONOGRAPH & SERIAL (008)

t	1998		lo#	a	g
Type of Date	Date1	Date2	Place of Publ.	Illustration	Target Audience

#						#	
Form Of Item	Nature of Contents	Govt. Pub.	Conf. Pub.	Festschrift	Index	Undefined	Literary Form

	eng	#	
Biography	Language	Modified Record	Cata. Source

NAME OF THE FIELD INCL. MARC21 TAG	INDICATORS 1	2	DATA WITH SUBFIELD IDENTIFIERS
ISBN NO. (020) (R)	#	#	$a 0878457162X $c
ISSN (022) (R)	#	#	$a
DEWEY DECIMAL CLASSIFICATION NUMBER (082) (R)	0	#	$a 823 $b 20th ed
MAIN ENTRY-PERSONAL NAME (100) (NR)			$a $b $c
MAIN ENTRY – CORPORATE NAME (110) (NR)		#	$a $b $c $d $n
MAIN ENTRY – MEETING NAME (111) (NR)		#	$a $c $d $e $n
MAIN ENTRY - UNIFORM TITLE (130) (NR)		#	$a $d $k $l $n
KEY TITLE(222)			$a $b
TITLA STATEMENT (245) (NR)			$a Collected fiction $b $c
EDITION STATEMENT (250) (nr)	#	#	$a 2nd ed $b
PUBLICATION DIST. ETC.(260) ®	3	#	$a London $b Penguin Books

			$c 1998
PHYSICAL DESC. (300) ®	#	#	$a 565p. $b ill. $c 22 cm. $e
SERIES STATEMENT/ ADDED ENTRY-TITLE (440) (R)	#		$a $n
SERIES STATEMENT (490)(R)		#	$a
GENERAL NOTE (500) (R)	#	#	$a Includes colour plates
CONTENTS NOTE (505) (R)		#	$a The Moon and the Sun/ by Anderi Tarkovsky. p. 11-25
SUBJECT ADDED ENTRY-PERSONAL NAME (600) (R)		0	$a $b $c
SUBJECT ADDED ENTRY-CORPORATE NAME (610) (R)		0	$a $c $d
SUBJECT ADDED ENTRY-TOPICAL NAME (650) (R)		0	$a English fiction $v $x $y $z
SUBJECT ADDED ENTRY-GEOGRAPHIC NAME (651) (R)	#	0	$a $v
ADDED ENTRY-PERSONAL NAME (700) (R)		#	$a Tarkovsky, Anderi, Borges, Luis Jorge, ed. $b $c
ADDED ENTRY-CORPORATE NAME (710) (R)		#	$a $b

			$c $d
ADDED ENTRY- MEETING NAME (711 (R)		#	$a $c $d
ADDED ENTRY – UNIFORM TITLE (730) (R)		#	$a
LOCATION (852)	1	#	$a
ACCESSION NO. INCL. DT. (901)			$a 18 $b 10-06-07 $c
CALL NO. (902)			$a 823N98
SUBJECT HEADING DEFINED BY (903)			$a S.Das
ENTERED BY (904)			$a S.Das
VERIFIED BY (905)			$a S.Das

NB. #= Put blank. R means Repeatable. NR means Not Repeatable

EXAMPLE 19

Collected Plays with preface

Third edition

Edited by

E. Thompson

Max Reinhardt Lourance

London

1979

O.I.: ISBN: 087-5497231-X / Page- 563 / Size - 23 cm. /
Contains - The nice man, by Nidssin Ezekiel, P. 131-140

MARC21: BIBLIOGRAPHIC FORMAT

LEADER (M):

n	a	m	a
Record Status	Type of record	Bibliographical level	Descriptive Catg.Form

CONTROL FIELD-MONOGRAPH & SERIAL (008)

t	1 9 7 9		1 o #	a	g
Type of Date	Date1	Date2	Place of Publ.	Illustration	Target Audience

#						#	
Form Of Item	Nature of Contents	Govt. Pub.	Conf. Pub.	Festschrift	Index	Undefined	Literary Form

	e n g	#	
Biography	Language	Modified Record	Cata. Source

NAME OF THE FIELD INCL. MARC21 TAG	INDICATORS 1	2	DATA WITH SUBFIELD IDENTIFIERS
ISBN NO. (020) (R)	#	#	$a 0875497231-X $c
ISSN (022) (R)	#	#	$a
DEWEY DECIMAL CLASSIFICATION NUMBER (082) (R)	0	#	$a 820.4195 $b 20th ed
MAIN ENTRY-PERSONAL NAME (100) (NR)			$a $b $c
MAIN ENTRY – CORPORATE NAME (110) (NR)		#	$a $b $c $d $n
MAIN ENTRY – MEETING NAME (111) (NR)		#	$a $c $d $e $n
MAIN ENTRY - UNIFORM TITLE (130) (NR)		#	$a $d $k $l $n
KEY TITLE(222)			$a $b
TITLA STATEMENT (245) (NR)			$a Collected plays with preface $b $c
EDITION STATEMENT (250) (nr)	#	#	$a 3rd ed $b

PUBLICATION DIST. ETC.(260) ®	3	#	$a London $b Max Reinhardt Lourance $c 1979
PHYSICAL DESC. (300) ®	#	#	$a 563p. $b col. : ill. $c 23 cm. $e
SERIES STATEMENT/ ADDED ENTRY-TITLE (440) (R)	#		$a $n
SERIES STATEMENT (490)(R)		#	$a
GENERAL NOTE (500) (R)	#	#	$a Includes author index. – This is the collection of English plays
CONTENTS NOTE (505) (R)		#	$a The nice man/ by Nidssin Ezekiel, p. 131-140
SUBJECT ADDED ENTRY-PERSONAL NAME (600) (R)		0	$a $b $c
SUBJECT ADDED ENTRY-CORPORATE NAME (610) (R)		0	$a $c $d
SUBJECT ADDED ENTRY-TOPICAL NAME (650) (R)		0	$a English plays $v $x $y $z
SUBJECT ADDED ENTRY-GEOGRAPHIC NAME (651) (R)	#	0	$a $v
ADDED ENTRY-PERSONAL NAME		#	$a Ezekiel, Nidssin, Thompson, E., <u>ed.</u>

(700) (R)			$b $c
ADDED ENTRY- CORPORATE NAME (710) (R)		#	$a $b $c $d
ADDED ENTRY- MEETING NAME (711 (R)		#	$a $c $d
ADDED ENTRY – UNIFORM TITLE (730) (R)		#	$a
LOCATION (852)	1	#	$a
ACCESSION NO. INCL. DT. (901)			$a 19 $b 10-06-07 $c
CALL NO. (902)			$a 820.4195L79
SUBJECT HEADING DEFINED BY (903)			$a S.Das
ENTERED BY (904)			$a S.Das
VERIFIED BY (905)			$a S.Das

NB. #= Put blank. R means Repeatable. NR means Not Repeatable

EXAMPLE20

Modern poetry
American and British

Edited by
K. FRIERAR

Appleton
New York

1951

O.I.: Contains colour illustration / Pages - 580 / Size - 22 cm. / Contains - Two sisters, by R. L. Stevenson. P. 1-2 / 4th Edition / ISBN: 08389-3156-1

MARC21: BIBLIOGRAPHIC FORMAT

LEADER (M):

Record Status	Type of record	Bibliographical level	Descriptive Catg.Form
n	a	m	a

CONTROL FIELD-MONOGRAPH & SERIAL (008)

Type of Date	Date1	Date2	Place of Publ.	Illustration	Target Audience
t	1 9 5 1		n y u	a	g

Form Of Item	Nature of Contents	Govt. Pub.	Conf. Pub.	Festschrift	Index	Undefined	Literary Form
#						#	

Biography	Language	Modified Record	Cata. Source
	e n g	#	

NAME OF THE FIELD INCL. MARC21 TAG	INDICATORS 1	2	DATA WITH SUBFIELD IDENTIFIERS
ISBN NO. (020) (R)	#	#	$a 0838931561 $c
ISSN (022) (R)	#	#	$a
DEWEY DECIMAL CLASSIFICATION NUMBER (082) (R)	0	#	$a 820.1542 $b 20th ed
MAIN ENTRY-PERSONAL NAME (100) (NR)			$a $b $c
MAIN ENTRY – CORPORATE NAME (110) (NR)		#	$a $b $c $d $n
MAIN ENTRY – MEETING NAME (111) (NR)		#	$a $c $d $e $n
MAIN ENTRY - UNIFORM TITLE (130) (NR)		#	$a $d $k $l $n
KEY TITLE(222)			$a $b
TITLA STATEMENT (245) (NR)			$a Modern poetry $b American and British $c
EDITION STATEMENT (250) (nr)	#	#	$a 4th ed $b
PUBLICATION DIST.	3	#	$a New York

ETC.(260) ®			$b Appleton $c 1951
PHYSICAL DESC. (300) ®	#	#	$a 580p. $b col. : ill. $c 22 cm. $e
SERIES STATEMENT/ ADDED ENTRY-TITLE (440) (R)	#		$a $n
SERIES STATEMENT (490)(R)		#	$a
GENERAL NOTE (500) (R)	#	#	$a Includes index. – This is the collection of English poetry
CONTENTS NOTE (505) (R)		#	$a Two sisters/ by R. L. Stevenson, p. 1-2
SUBJECT ADDED ENTRY-PERSONAL NAME (600) (R)		0	$a $b $c
SUBJECT ADDED ENTRY-CORPORATE NAME (610) (R)		0	$a $c $d
SUBJECT ADDED ENTRY-TOPICAL NAME (650) (R)		0	$a English poetry $v $x $y $z
SUBJECT ADDED ENTRY-GEOGRAPHIC NAME (651) (R)	#	0	$a $v
ADDED ENTRY- PERSONAL NAME (700) (R)		#	$a Stevenson, R.L., Frierar, K., ed. $b $c
ADDED ENTRY- CORPORATE NAME (710) (R)		#	$a $b

			$c $d
ADDED ENTRY- MEETING NAME (711 (R)		#	$a $c $d
ADDED ENTRY – UNIFORM TITLE (730) (R)		#	$a
LOCATION (852)	1	#	$a
ACCESSION NO. INCL. DT. (901)			$a 20 $b 10-06-07 $c
CALL NO. (902)			$a 820.1542J51
SUBJECT HEADING DEFINED BY (903)			$a S.Das
ENTERED BY (904)			$a S.Das
VERIFIED BY (905)			$a S.Das

NB. #= Put blank. R means Repeatable. NR means Not Repeatable

5

MARC 21: Bibliographic Format of Corporate Body

EXAMPLE 21

REPORT OF ADVISORY
COMMITTEE FOR LIBRARIES

1959

MINISTRY OF EDUCATION

Government of India

O.I. – Shri K. P. Sinha was the chairman of the committee. The work is 'also known as Sinha Committee Report.'/Back of the title page: Published by the Manager of Publications, Delhi. Published in 1959./144 Pages /Size: 23 x 14 cm.

MARC21: BIBLIOGRAPHIC FORMAT

LEADER (M):

Record Status	Type of record	Bibliographical level	Descriptive Catg.Form
n	a	m	a

CONTROL FIELD-MONOGRAPH & SERIAL (008)

Type of Date	Date1	Date2	Place of Publ.	Illustration	Target Audience
t	1 9 5 9		d e i		g

Form Of Item	Nature of Contents	Govt. Pub.	Conf. Pub.	Festschrift	Index	Undefined	Literary Form
#		o				#	

Biography	Language	Modified Record	Cata. Source
	e n g	#	

NAME OF THE FIELD INCL. MARC21 TAG	INDICATORS 1	2	DATA WITH SUBFIELD IDENTIFIERS
ISBN NO. (020) (R)	#	#	$a 0838931562 $c
ISSN (022) (R)	#	#	$a
DEWEY DECIMAL CLASSIFICATION NUMBER (082) (R)	0	#	$a 027.0954 $b 20th ed
MAIN ENTRY-PERSONAL NAME (100) (NR)			$a $b $c
MAIN ENTRY –CORPORATE NAME (110) (NR)		#	$a India $b Ministry of Education $c $d $n
MAIN ENTRY – MEETING NAME (111) (NR)		#	$a $c $d $e $n
MAIN ENTRY - UNIFORM TITLE (130) (NR)		#	$a $d $k $l $n
KEY TITLE(222)			$a $b
TITLA STATEMENT (245) (NR)			$a Report of advisory committee for libraries $b $c
EDITION STATEMENT (250) (nr)	#	#	$a $b

PUBLICATION DIST. ETC.(260) ®	3	#	$a Delhi $b Manager of Publications $c 1959
PHYSICAL DESC. (300) ®	#	#	$a 141p. $b $c 23 cm. $e
SERIES STATEMENT/ ADDED ENTRY-TITLE (440) (R)	#		$a $n
SERIES STATEMENT (490)(R)		#	$a
GENERAL NOTE (500) (R)	#	#	$a K.P. Sinha, Chairman, Advisory Committee for Libraries. - Also known as Sinha Committee Report.
CONTENTS NOTE (505)(R)		#	$a
SUBJECT ADDED ENTRY- PERSONAL NAME (600) (R)		0	$a $b $c
SUBJECT ADDED ENTRY- CORPORATE NAME (610) (R)		0	$a $c $d
SUBJECT ADDED ENTRY- TOPICAL NAME (650) (R)		0	$a Libraries $v $x $y $z India
SUBJECT ADDED ENTRY- GEOGRAPHIC NAME (651) (R)	#	0	$a $v
ADDED ENTRY- PERSONAL NAME (700) (R)		#	$a $b $c

ADDED ENTRY- CORPORATE NAME (710) (R)		#	$a $b $c $d
ADDED ENTRY- MEETING NAME (711 (R)		#	$a $c $d
ADDED ENTRY – UNIFORM TITLE (730) (R)		#	$a
LOCATION (852)	1	#	$a
ACCESSION NO. INCL. DT. (901)			$a 21 $b 6-10-07 $c
CALL NO. (902)			$a 027.0954 J59
SUBJECT HEADING DEFINED BY (903)			$a S.Das
ENTERED BY (904)			$a S.Das
VERIFIED BY (905)			$a S.Das

NB. #= Put blank. R means Repeatable. NR means Not Repeatable

EXAMPLE 22

ORGAN OF A GOVERNMENT
FOURTH GENERAL ELECTIONS : AN ANALYSIS
MINISTRY OF INFORMATION & BROADCASTING

Government of India

1971

O.I. — xi, 120 Pages/ Size: 25 cm. / Back of the title page: Published by the Manager of Publications, New Delhi. Published in 1971.

MARC21: BIBLIOGRAPHIC FORMAT

LEADER (M):

Record Status	Type of record	Bibliographical level	Descriptive Catg.Form
n	a	m	a

CONTROL FIELD-MONOGRAPH & SERIAL (008)

Type of Date	Date1	Date2	Place of Publ.	Illustration	Target Audience
t	1 9 7 1		n e i		g

Form Of Item	Nature of Contents	Govt. Pub.	Conf. Pub.	Festschrift	Index	Undefined	Literary Form
#		o				#	

Biography	Language	Modified Record	Cata. Source
	e n g	#	

NAME OF THE FIELD INCL. MARC21 TAG	INDICATORS 1	2	DATA WITH SUBFIELD IDENTIFIERS
ISBN NO. (020) (R)	#	#	$a $c
ISSN (022) (R)	#	#	$a
DEWEY DECIMAL CLASSIFICATION NUMBER (082) (R)	0	#	$a 324.0954 $b 20th ed
MAIN ENTRY-PERSONAL NAME (100) (NR)			$a $b $c
MAIN ENTRY – CORPORATE NAME (110) (NR)		#	$a India $b Ministry of Information and Broadcasting $c $d $n
MAIN ENTRY – MEETING NAME (111) (NR)		#	$a $c $d $e $n
MAIN ENTRY - UNIFORM TITLE (130) (NR)		#	$a $d $k $l $n
KEY TITLE(222)			$a $b
TITLA STATEMENT (245) (NR)			$a Fourth general elections $b an analysis $c

EDITION STATEMENT (250) (nr)	#	#	$a $b
PUBLICATION DIST. ETC.(260) ®	3	#	$a New Delhi $b Manager of Publications $c 1971
PHYSICAL DESC. (300) ®	#	#	$a xi, 120 p. $b $c 25 cm. $e
SERIES STATEMENT/ ADDED ENTRY-TITLE (440) (R)	#		$a $n
SERIES STATEMENT (490)(R)		#	$a
GENERAL NOTE (500) (R)	#	#	$a
CONTENTS NOTE (505)(R)		#	$a
SUBJECT ADDED ENTRY-PERSONAL NAME (600) (R)		0	$a $b $c
SUBJECT ADDED ENTRY-CORPORATE NAME (610) (R)		0	$a $c $d
SUBJECT ADDED ENTRY-TOPICAL NAME (650) (R)		0	$a Elections $v $x $y $z India
SUBJECT ADDED ENTRY-GEOGRAPHIC NAME (651) (R)	#	0	$a $v
ADDED ENTRY-PERSONAL NAME (700) (R)		#	$a $b $c
ADDED ENTRY-		#	$a

CORPORATE NAME (710) (R)			$b $c $d
ADDED ENTRY- MEETING NAME (711 (R)		#	$a $c $d
ADDED ENTRY – UNIFORM TITLE (730) (R)		#	$a
LOCATION (852)	1	#	$a
ACCESSION NO. INCL. DT. (901)			$a 22 $b 6-10-07 $c
CALL NO. (902)			$a 324.0954 L71
SUBJECT HEADING DEFINED BY (903)			$a S.Das
ENTERED BY (904)			$a S.Das
VERIFIED BY (905)			$a S.Das

NB. #= Put blank. R means Repeatable. NR means Not Repeatable

EXAMPLE 23

Government Publication :information about authorship taken from preface, series.

THE BRITISH SYSTEM OF TAXATION

HER MAJESTY'S STATIONERY OFFICE LONDON

1956

O.I. — The pamphlet was prepared by Reference Division, Central Office of Information./41 volume/ Size : 24 x 14 cm./ Half title page : Central Office of Information. Reference pamphlet, 10.

MARC21: BIBLIOGRAPHIC FORMAT

LEADER (M):

Record Status	Type of record	Bibliographical level	Descriptive Catg.Form
n	a	m	a

CONTROL FIELD-MONOGRAPH & SERIAL (008)

Type of Date	Date1	Date2	Place of Publ.	Illustration	Target Audience
t	1 9 5 6		l o #		g

Form Of Item	Nature of Contents	Govt. Pub.	Conf. Pub.	Festschrift	Index	Undefined	Literary Form
#		o				#	

Biography	Language	Modified Record	Cata. Source
	e n g	#	

NAME OF THE FIELD INCL. MARC21 TAG	INDICATORS 1	2	DATA WITH SUBFIELD IDENTIFIERS
ISBN NO. (020) (R)	#	#	$a $c
ISSN (022) (R)	#	#	$a
DEWEY DECIMAL CLASSIFICATION NUMBER (082) (R)	0	#	$a 336.209 41 $b 20th ed
MAIN ENTRY-PERSONAL NAME (100) (NR)			$a $b $c
MAIN ENTRY – CORPORATE NAME (110) (NR)		#	$a London $b Her Majesty's Stationery Office $c $d $n
MAIN ENTRY – MEETING NAME (111) (NR)		#	$a $c $d $e $n
MAIN ENTRY - UNIFORM TITLE (130) (NR)		#	$a $d $k $l $n
KEY TITLE(222)			$a $b
TITLA STATEMENT (245) (NR)			$a The British system of taxation $b $c
EDITION STATEMENT (250) (nr)	#	#	$a $b

PUBLICATION DIST. ETC.(260) ®	3	#	$a London $b Her Majesty's Stationery Office $c 1956
PHYSICAL DESC. (300) ®	#	#	$a v, 41 p. $b $c 24 cm. $e
SERIES STATEMENT/ ADDED ENTRY-TITLE (440) (R)	#		$a [Gt. Brit.] Central Office of Information Reference Pamphlet $n 10
SERIES STATEMENT (490)(R)		#	$a
GENERAL NOTE (500) (R)	#	#	$a
CONTENTS NOTE (505)(R)		#	$a
SUBJECT ADDED ENTRY- PERSONAL NAME (600) (R)		0	$a $b $c
SUBJECT ADDED ENTRY- CORPORATE NAME (610) (R)		0	$a $c $d
SUBJECT ADDED ENTRY- TOPICAL NAME (650) (R)		0	$a Taxation $v $x $y $z Great Britain
SUBJECT ADDED ENTRY- GEOGRAPHIC NAME (651) (R)	#	0	$a $v
ADDED ENTRY- PERSONAL NAME (700) (R)		#	$a $b $c

ADDED ENTRY- CORPORATE NAME (710) (R)		#	$a $b $c $d
ADDED ENTRY- MEETING NAME (711 (R)		#	$a $c $d
ADDED ENTRY – UNIFORM TITLE (730) (R)		#	$a
LOCATION (852)	1	#	$a
ACCESSION NO. INCL. DT. (901)			$a 23 $b 6-10-07 $c
CALL NO. (902)			$a 336.209 41J56
SUBJECT HEADING DEFINED BY (903)			$a S.Das
ENTERED BY (904)			$a S.Das
VERIFIED BY (905)			$a S.Das

NB. #= Put blank. R means Repeatable. NR means Not Repeatable

EXAMPLE 24

Government Publication: Part of title given within Parenthesis.

THE CONSTITUTION OF INDIA

(as modified up to 1st April 1958)

DelhiMANAGER OF PUBLICATIONS

1958

O.I.—327 Pages/ Size : 19 x 12 cm

MARC21: BIBLIOGRAPHIC FORMAT

LEADER (M):

Record Status	Type of record	Bibliographical level	Descriptive Catg.Form
n	a	m	a

CONTROL FIELD-MONOGRAPH & SERIAL (008)

Type of Date	Date1	Date2	Place of Publ.	Illustration	Target Audience
t	1 9 5 8		d e i		g

Form Of Item	Nature of Contents	Govt. Pub.	Conf. Pub.	Festschrift	Index	Undefined	Literary Form
#		o				#	

Biography	Language	Modified Record	Cata. Source
	e n g	#	

NAME OF THE FIELD INCL. MARC21 TAG	INDICATORS 1	2	DATA WITH SUBFIELD IDENTIFIERS
ISBN NO. (020) (R)	#	#	$a $c
ISSN (022) (R)	#	#	$a
DEWEY DECIMAL CLASSIFICATION NUMBER (082) (R)	0	#	$a 342.095 4 $b 20th ed
MAIN ENTRY-PERSONAL NAME (100) (NR)			$a $b $c
MAIN ENTRY –CORPORATE NAME (110) (NR)		#	$a India $b Delhi $c Manager of Publications. $d $n
MAIN ENTRY – MEETING NAME (111) (NR)		#	$a $c $d $e $n
MAIN ENTRY - UNIFORM TITLE (130) (NR)		#	$a $d $k $l $n
KEY TITLE(222)			$a $b
TITLA STATEMENT (245) (NR)			$a The Constitution of India (as modified up to 1st April 1958). $b $c

EDITION STATEMENT (250) (nr)	#	#	$a $b
PUBLICATION DIST. ETC.(260) ®	3	#	$a Delhi $b Manager of Publication $c 1958
PHYSICAL DESC. (300) ®	#	#	$a 327 p. $b 19 cm. $c $e
SERIES STATEMENT/ ADDED ENTRY-TITLE (440) (R)	#		$a $n
SERIES STATEMENT (490)(R)		#	$a
GENERAL NOTE (500) (R)	#	#	$a
CONTENTS NOTE (505)(R)		#	$a
SUBJECT ADDED ENTRY-PERSONAL NAME (600) (R)		0	$a $b $c
SUBJECT ADDED ENTRY-CORPORATE NAME (610) (R)		0	$a $c $d
SUBJECT ADDED ENTRY-TOPICAL NAME (650) (R)		0	$a Constitution $v $x $y $z India
SUBJECT ADDED ENTRY-GEOGRAPHIC NAME (651) (R)	#	0	$a $v
ADDED ENTRY-PERSONAL NAME (700) (R)		#	$a $b $c
ADDED ENTRY-		#	$a

CORPORATE NAME (710) (R)			$b $c $d
ADDED ENTRY- MEETING NAME (711 (R)		#	$a $c $d
ADDED ENTRY – UNIFORM TITLE (730) (R)		#	$a
LOCATION (852)	1	#	$a
ACCESSION NO. INCL. DT. (901)			$a 24 $b 6-10-07 $c
CALL NO. (902)			$a 342.095 4J58
SUBJECT HEADING DEFINED BY (903)			$a S.Das
ENTERED BY (904)			$a S.Das
VERIFIED BY (905)			$a S.Das

NB. #= Put blank. R means Repeatable. NR means Not Repeatable

EXAMPLE 25

Organ of a government
(*Administration Unit*)

HISTORY OF MADHYA PRADESH POLICE

POLICE DEPARTMENT
MADHYA PRADESH

1965

O.I.—Volume 393 and 40 pages /Size: 25 cm. /Back of the title page: Published by the Inspector General of Police (M.P.), Bhopal. Published in 1965.

MARC21: BIBLIOGRAPHIC FORMAT

LEADER (M):

n	a	m	a
Record Status	Type of record	Bibliographical level	Descriptive Catg.Form

CONTROL FIELD-MONOGRAPH & SERIAL (008)

t		b h i		g
Type of Date	Date1	Date2	Place of Publ.	Illustration	Target Audience

#	1 9 6 5	o				#	
Form Of Item	Nature of Contents	Govt. Pub.	Conf. Pub.	Festschrift	Index	Undefined	Literary Form

	e n g	#	
Biography	Language	Modified Record	Cata. Source

NAME OF THE FIELD INCL. MARC21 TAG	INDICATORS 1	2	DATA WITH SUBFIELD IDENTIFIERS
ISBN NO. (020) (R)	#	#	$a $c
ISSN (022) (R)	#	#	$a
DEWEY DECIMAL CLASSIFICATION NUMBER (082) (R)	0	#	$a 363.209 54 $b 20th ed
MAIN ENTRY-PERSONAL NAME (100) (NR)			$a $b $c
MAIN ENTRY –CORPORATE NAME (110) (NR)		#	$a Madhya Pradesh $b Police Department $c $d $n
MAIN ENTRY – MEETING NAME (111) (NR)		#	$a $c $d $e $n
MAIN ENTRY - UNIFORM TITLE (130) (NR)		#	$a $d $k $l $n
KEY TITLE(222)			$a $b
TITLA STATEMENT (245) (NR)			$a History of Madhya Pradesh Police $b $c
EDITION STATEMENT (250) (nr)	#	#	$a $b

PUBLICATION DIST. ETC.(260) ®	3	#	$a Bhopal $b Inspector General of Police (M.P.) $c 1965
PHYSICAL DESC. (300) ®	#	#	$a v, 433 p. $b $c 25 cm. $e
SERIES STATEMENT/ ADDED ENTRY-TITLE (440) (R)	#		$a $n
SERIES STATEMENT (490)(R)		#	$a
GENERAL NOTE (500) (R)	#	#	$a
CONTENTS NOTE (505)(R)		#	$a
SUBJECT ADDED ENTRY-PERSONAL NAME (600) (R)		0	$a $b $c
SUBJECT ADDED ENTRY-CORPORATE NAME (610) (R)		0	$a $c $d
SUBJECT ADDED ENTRY-TOPICAL NAME (650) (R)		0	$a Police $v $x $y $z Madhya Pradesh
SUBJECT ADDED ENTRY-	#	0	$a
GEOGRAPHIC NAME (651) (R)			$v
ADDED ENTRY- PERSONAL NAME (700) (R)		#	$a $b $c
ADDED ENTRY-CORPORATE NAME		#	$a $b

(710) (R)			$c $d
ADDED ENTRY- MEETING NAME (711 (R)		#	$a $c $d
ADDED ENTRY – UNIFORM TITLE (730) (R)		#	$a
LOCATION (852)	1	#	$a
ACCESSION NO. INCL. DT. (901)			$a 25 $b 6-10-07 $c
CALL NO. (902)			$a 363.209 54K65
SUBJECT HEADING DEFINED BY (903)			$a S.Das
ENTERED BY (904)			$a S.Das
VERIFIED BY (905)			$a S.Das

NB. #= Put blank. R means Repeatable. NR means Not Repeatable

EXAMPLE 26

Judgment of the International Court of Justice

For the

Right of passage over Indian territory

(*Kashmir and Srinagar Case*)

Delivered on the

15 December 1992

New Delhi

Ministry of External Affairs, Government of India

O.I.—Three preliminary pages in Roman number and 85 pages in Arabic numbered/ Size:28 cm

MARC21: BIBLIOGRAPHIC FORMAT

LEADER (M):

Record Status	Type of record	Bibliographical level	Descriptive Catg.Form
n	a	m	a

....

CONTROL FIELD-MONOGRAPH & SERIAL (008)

Type of Date	Date1	Date2	Place of Publ.	Illustration	Target Audience
t	1992		ndi		f

Form Of Item	Nature of Contents	Govt. Pub.	Conf. Pub.	Festschrift	Index	Undefined	Literary Form
#		#				#	

Biography	Language	Modified Record	Cata. Source
	eng	#	

....

NAME OF THE FIELD INCL. MARC21 TAG	INDICATORS 1	2	DATA WITH SUBFIELD IDENTIFIERS
ISBN NO. (020) (R)	#	#	$a $c
ISSN (022) (R)	#	#	$a
DEWEY DECIMAL CLASSIFICATION NUMBER (082) (R)	0	#	$a 341 $b 20th ed
MAIN ENTRY-PERSONAL NAME (100) (NR)	#	#	$a $b $c
MAIN ENTRY – CORPORATE NAME (110) NR	1	#	$a International Court of Justice $b $c $d $n
MAIN ENTRY – MEETING name (111) (NR)	#	#	$a $c $d $e $n
MAIN ENTRY - UNIFORM TITLE (130) (NR)		#	$a $d $k $l $n
TITLA STATEMENT (245) (NR)	1	#	$a Right of passage over Indian territory (Kashmir and Srinagar case) $b $c
EDITION STATEMENT (250) (nr)	#	#	$a $b

PUBLICATION DIST. ETC.(260) ®	3	#	$a New Delhi $b Ministry of External Affairs $c 1992
PHYSICAL DESC. (300) ®	#	#	$a iii, 85p. $b $c 28 cm. $e
SERIES STATEMENT/ ADDED ENTRY-TITLE (440) (R)	#		$a $n
SERIES STATEMENT (490)(R)	#	#	$a
GENERAL NOTE (500) (R)	#	#	$a
CONTENTS NOTE (505)(R)		#	$a
SUBJECT ADDED ENTRY-PERSONAL NAME (600) (R)			$a $b $c
SUBJECT ADDED ENTRY-CORPORATE NAME (610) (R)			$a $c $d
SUBJECT ADDED ENTRY-TOPICAL NAME (650) (R)		0	$a International law $v $x $y $z
SUBJECT ADDED ENTRY-GEOGRAPHIC NAME (651) (R)			$a $v
ADDED ENTRY- PERSONAL NAME (700) (R)			$a $b $c
ADDED ENTRY- CORPORATE NAME (710) (R)			$a $b $c $d

ADDED ENTRY- MEETING NAME (711 (R)			$a $c $d
ADDED ENTRY – UNIFORM TITLE (730) (R)			$a
LOCATION (852)	1	#	$a
ACCESSION NO. INCL. DT. (901)			$a 26 $b 6-10-07 $c
CALL NO. (902)			$a 341N92
SUBJECT HEADING DEFINED BY (903)			$a S.Das
ENTERED BY (904)			$a S.Das
VERIFIED BY (905)			$a S.Das

NB. #= Put blank. R means Repeatable. NR means Not Repeatable

EXAMPLE 27

GOVERNMENT OF INDIA
MINISTRY OF EDUCATION

Organisation of Training System
& Educational Manual

Illustrated by
Manager of Publications
New Delhi

1993

O. I.– 990 Pages/ Size: 28 cm./ Note: It is publication No. 93 of the Ministry of Education Publication Series.

MARC21: BIBLIOGRAPHIC FORMAT

LEADER (M):

Record Status	Type of record	Bibliographical level	Descriptive Catg.Form
n	a	m	a

CONTROL FIELD-MONOGRAPH & SERIAL (008)

Type of Date	Date1	Date2	Place of Publ.	Illustration	Target Audience
t	1 9 9 3		n d i		g

Form Of Item	Nature of Contents	Govt. Pub.	Conf. Pub.	Festschrift	Index	Undefined	Literary Form
#		o				#	

Biography	Language	Modified Record	Cata. Source
	e n g	#	

NAME OF THE FIELD INCL. MARC21 TAG	INDICATORS 1	2	DATA WITH SUBFIELD IDENTIFIERS
ISBN NO. (020) (R)	#	#	$a $c
ISSN (022) (R)	#	#	$a
DEWEY DECIMAL CLASSIFICATION NUMBER (082) (R)	0	#	$a 371 $b 20th ed
MAIN ENTRY-PERSONAL NAME (100) (NR)			$a $b $c
MAIN ENTRY –CORPORATE NAME (110) NR		#	$a India $b Ministry of Education $c $d $n
MAIN ENTRY – MEETING NAME (111) (NR)		#	$a $c $d $e $n
MAIN ENTRY - UNIFORM TITLE (130) (NR)		#	$a $d $k $l $n
TITLA STATEMENT (245) (NR)			$a Organisation of training system & educational manual $b $c
EDITION STATEMENT (250) (nr)	#	#	$a $b
PUBLICATION DIST. ETC.(260) ®	3	#	$a New Delhi $b Manager of

			Publications $c 1993
PHYSICAL DESC. (300) ®	#	#	$a 990p. $b $c 28 cm. $e
SERIES STATEMENT/ ADDED ENTRY-TITLE (440) (R)	#		$a $n
SERIES STATEMENT (490)(R)		#	$a
GENERAL NOTE (500) (R)	#	#	$a It is publication no. 93 of the Ministry of Education Publication Series
CONTENTS NOTE (505)(R)		#	$a
SUBJECT ADDED ENTRY- PERSONAL NAME (600) (R)		0	$a $b $c
SUBJECT ADDED ENTRY- CORPORATE NAME (610) (R)		0	$a $c $d
SUBJECT ADDED ENTRY- TOPICAL NAME (650) (R)		0	$a Education $v Training manual, Manual $x $y $z
SUBJECT ADDED ENTRY- GEOGRAPHIC NAME (651) (R)	#	0	$a $v
ADDED ENTRY- PERSONAL NAME (700) (R)		#	$a $b $c

ADDED ENTRY- CORPORATE NAME (710) (R)		#	$a $b $c $d
ADDED ENTRY- MEETING NAME (711 (R)		#	$a $c $d
ADDED ENTRY – UNIFORM TITLE (730) (R)		#	$a
LOCATION (852)	1	#	$a
ACCESSION NO. INCL. DT. (901)			$a 27 $b 6-10-07 $c
CALL NO. (902)			$a 371 N93
SUBJECT HEADING DEFINED BY (903)			$a S.Das
ENTERED BY (904)			$a S.Das
VERIFIED BY (905)			$a S.Das

NB. #= Put blank. R means Repeatable. NR means Not Repeatable

EXAMPLE 28

ADULT EDUCATION IN INDIA

Report of the Assessment Committee on Adult Education.

(*Ministry of Education*)

Government of India,

Manager of Publications

New Delhi

1993

O.I.– 705 Pages/ Size : 28 cm./Note :This report is only for elementary education for adult.

MARC21: BIBLIOGRAPHIC FORMAT

LEADER (M):

Record	Type of Status	Bibliographical record	Descriptive Catg.Form level
n	a	m	a

CONTROL FIELD-MONOGRAPH & SERIAL (008)

Type of Date	Date1	Date2	Place of Publ.	Illustration	Target Audience
t	1 9 9 3		n d i		g

Form Of Item	Nature of Contents	Govt. Pub.	Conf. Pub.	Festschrift	Index	Undefined	Literary Form
#		o				#	

Biography	Language	Modified Record	Cata. Source
	e n g	#	

NAME OF THE FIELD INCL. MARC21 TAG	INDICATORS 1	2	DATA WITH SUBFIELD IDENTIFIERS
ISBN NO. (020) (R)	#	#	$a $c
ISSN (022) (R)	#	#	$a
DEWEY DECIMAL CLASSIFICATION NUMBER (082) (R)	0	#	$a 374.7 $b 20th ed
MAIN ENTRY-PERSONAL NAME (100) (NR)			$a $b $c
MAIN ENTRY – CORPORATE NAME (110) NR		#	$a India $b Ministry of Education $c Assessment Committee on Adult Education $d $n
MAIN ENTRY – MEETING name (111) (NR)		#	$a $c $d $e $n
MAIN ENTRY - UNIFORM TITLE (130) (NR)		#	$a $d $k $l $n
TITLA STATEMENT (245) (NR)			$a Adult education in India $b $c
EDITION STATEMENT (250) (nr)	#	#	$a $b

PUBLICATION DIST. ETC.(260) ®	3	#	$a New Delhi $b Manager of Publications $c 1993
PHYSICALDESC. (300) ®	#	#	$a 705p. $b $c 28 cm. $e
SERIES STATEMENT/ ADDED ENTRY-TITLE (440) (R)	#		$a $n
SERIES STATEMENT (490)(R)		#	$a
GENERAL NOTE (500) (R)	#	#	$a This report is only for elementary education for adult
CONTENTS NOTE (505)(R)		#	$a
SUBJECT ADDED ENTRY- PERSONAL NAME (600) (R)		0	$a $b $c
SUBJECT ADDED ENTRY- CORPORATE NAME (610) (R)		0	$a $c $d
SUBJECT ADDED ENTRY- TOPICAL NAME (650) (R)		0	$a Education $v Elementary $x $y $z
SUBJECT ADDED ENTRY- GEOGRAPHIC NAME (651) (R)	#	0	$a $v
ADDED ENTRY- PERSONAL NAME (700) (R)		#	$a $b $c
ADDED ENTRY- CORPORATE NAME (710) (R)		#	$a $b

			$c $d
ADDED ENTRY- MEETING NAME (711 (R)		#	$a $c $d
ADDED ENTRY – UNIFORM TITLE (730) (R)		#	$a
LOCATION (852)	1	#	$a
ACCESSION NO. INCL. DT. (901)			$a 28 $b 6-10-07 $c
CALL NO. (902)			$a 347.7N93
SUBJECT HEADING DEFINED BY (903)			$a S.Das
ENTERED BY (904)			$a S.Das
VERIFIED BY (905)			$a S.Das

NB. #= Put blank. R means Repeatable. NR means Not Repeatable

6

MARC 21: Bibliographic Format of Uniform Titles

EXAMPLE 29

The Bhagavad-Gita
Annie Besant with an essay on The Gita

By
Parthasarathy

Collected and edited by
Santi L. Mukerjee, Hitendra Mitra

Text in English and Sanskrit
Orbit Publications

Calcutta

1991

O. I: The Book has twenty-one preliminary pages and 259 pages in Arabic numerals. The height of the book is 22 cm. ISBN – 0-521-439809(pbk). Accession No. – 28672

MARC21: BIBLIOGRAPHIC FORMAT

LEADER (M):

n	a	m	a
Record Status	Type of record	Bibliographical level	Descriptive Catg.Form

CONTROL FIELD-MONOGRAPH & SERIAL (008)

t	1 9 9 1		c a i		g
Type of Date	Date1	Date2	Place of Publ.	Illustration	Target Audience

#						#	
Form Of Item	Nature of Contents	Govt. Pub.	Conf. Pub.	Festschrift	Index	Undefined	Literary Form

	e n g	#	
Biography	Language	Modified Record	Cata. Source

NAME OF THE FIELD INCL. MARC21 TAG	INDICATORS 1	2	DATA WITH SUBFIELD IDENTIFIERS
ISBN NO. (020) (R)	#	#	$a 0521-43980-9 (pbk.) $c
ISSN (022) (R)	#	#	$a
DEWEY DECIMAL CLASSIFICATION NUMBER (082) (R)	0	#	$a 294.5/924 $b 20th ed
MAIN ENTRY-PERSONAL NAME (100) (NR)			$a $b $c
MAIN ENTRY –CORPORATE NAME (110) NR		#	$a $b $c $d $n
MAIN ENTRY – MEETING name (111) (NR)		#	$a $c $d $e $n
MAIN ENTRY - UNIFORM TITLE (130) (NR)		#	$a Bhagavad-Gita $d $k $l English & Sanskrit $n
TITLA STATEMENT (245) (NR)			$a The Bhagavad-Gita $b $c Annie Besant; with an essay on The Gita by A. Parthasarathy; collected and edited by Santi L. Mukherjee, Hitenra Mitra

EDITION STATEMENT (250) (nr)	#	#	$a $b
PUBLICATION DIST. ETC.(260) ®	3	#	$a Calcutta $b Orbit Publications $c 1991
PHYSICAL DESC. (300) ®	#	#	$a xxi, 259p. $b $c 22cm. $e
SERIES STATEMENT/ ADDED ENTRY-TITLE (440) (R)	#		$a $n
SERIES STATEMENT (490)(R)		#	$a
GENERAL NOTE (500) (R)	#	#	$a English & Sanskrit
CONTENTS NOTE (505)(R)		#	$a
SUBJECT ADDED ENTRY-PERSONAL NAME (600) (R)		0	$a $b $c
SUBJECT ADDED ENTRY-CORPORATE NAME (610) (R)		0	$a $c $d
SUBJECT ADDED ENTRY-TOPICAL NAME (650) (R)		0	$a $v $x $y $z
SUBJECT ADDED ENTRY-GEOGRAPHIC NAME (651) (R)	#	0	$a $v
ADDED ENTRY- PERSONAL NAME (700) (R)		#	$a Besant, Annie , Parthasarathy, A. , Mukherjee, Santi L. , Mitra, Hirendra $b

			$c
ADDED ENTRY- CORPORATE NAME (710) (R)		#	$a $b $c $d
ADDED ENTRY- MEETING NAME (711 (R)		#	$a $c $d
ADDED ENTRY – UNIFORM TITLE (730) (R)		#	$a
LOCATION (852)	1	#	$a
ACCESSION NO. INCL. DT. (901)			$a 29 $b 6-10-07 $c
CALL NO. (902)			$a 294.5/924 N91
SUBJECT HEADING DEFINED BY (903)			$a S.Das
ENTERED BY (904)			$a S.Das
VERIFIED BY (905)			$a S.Das

NB. #= Put blank. R means Repeatable. NR means Not Repeatable

EXAMPLE 30

The Ramayana of Valmiki
An epic of an Epic of ancient India

Introduced and Translated
by
Robert P. Goldman and Sally J. Sutherl
and Text in English Selections

Oxford University Press
(Delhi / Bombay / Calcutta / Madras)
copyright 1984

O. I: The book has sixteen preliminary pages numbered in Roman numerals, 384 tcxtual pages including illustrations. Height: 22 cm. ISBN – 0-471-02695-6. Accession no. – 2354B. T. P: Reprinted of the 1900 ed. Published by J. M. Dent, London.

MARC21: BIBLIOGRAPHIC FORMAT

LEADER (M):

Record Status	Type of record	Bibliographical level	Descriptive Catg.Form
n	a	m	a

CONTROL FIELD-MONOGRAPH & SERIAL (008)

Type of Date	Date1	Date2	Place of Publ.	Illustration	Target Audience
t	1 9 8 4		d e i	a	g

Form Of Item	Nature of Contents	Govt. Pub.	Conf. Pub.	Festschrift	Index	Undefined	Literary Form
#						#	

Biography	Language	Modified Record	Cata. Source
	e n g	#	

NAME OF THE FIELD INCL. MARC21 TAG	INDICATORS 1	2	DATA WITH SUBFIELD IDENTIFIERS
ISBN NO. (020) (R) 3	#	#	$a 0-471-02695-6 $c
ISSN (022) (R)	#	#	$a
DEWEY DECIMAL CLASSIFICATION NUMBER (082) (R)	0	#	$a 294.5/922 $b 20th ed
MAIN ENTRY-PERSONAL NAME (100) (NR)			$a $b $c
MAIN ENTRY – CORPORATE NAME (110) NR		#	$a $b $c $d $n
MAIN ENTRY – MEETING name (111) (NR)		#	$a $c $d $e $n
MAIN ENTRY - UNIFORM TITLE (130) (NR)		#	$a Valmiki $d $k Ramayana $l English $n Selections
TITLA STATEMENT (245) (NR)			$a The Ramayana of Valmiki $b an epic of ancient India $c introduced and translated by Robert P. Goldman and Sally J. Sutherland
EDITION STATEMENT	#	#	$a

(250) (nr)			$b
PUBLICATION DIST. ETC.(260) ®	3	#	$a Delhi $b Oxford University Press $c c1984
PHYSICAL DESC. (300) ®	#	#	$a xvi, 384p. $b ill. $c 22 cm. $e
SERIES STATEMENT/ ADDED ENTRY-TITLE (440) (R)	#		$a $n
SERIES STATEMENT (490)(R)		#	$a
GENERAL NOTE (500) (R)	#	#	$a Reprint of the 1900 ed. Published by J.M. Dent, London
CONTENTS NOTE (505) (R)		#	$a
SUBJECT ADDED ENTRY- PERSONAL NAME (600) (R)		0	$a Goldman, Robert P. , Sutherland, Sally J. $b $c
SUBJECT ADDED ENTRY- CORPORATE NAME (610) (R)		0	$a $c $d
SUBJECT ADDED ENTRY- TOPICAL NAME (650) (R)		0	$a $v $x $y $z
SUBJECT ADDED ENTRY- GEOGRAPHIC NAME (651) (R)	#	0	$a $v
ADDED ENTRY- PERSONAL NAME		#	$a $b

(700) (R)			$c
ADDED ENTRY- CORPORATE NAME (710) (R)		#	$a $b $c $d
ADDED ENTRY- MEETING NAME (711 (R)		#	$a $c $d
ADDED ENTRY – UNIFORM TITLE (730) (R)		#	$a
LOCATION (852)	1	#	$a
ACCESSION NO. INCL. DT. (901)			$a 30 $b 6-10-07 $c
CALL NO. (902)			$a 294.5/922 M84
SUBJECT HEADING DEFINED BY (903)			$a S.Das
ENTERED BY (904)			$a S.Das
VERIFIED BY (905)			$a S.Das

NB. #= Put blank. R means Repeatable. NR means Not Repeatable

EXAMPLE31

Hymns of the Atharva-Veda
(Together with extracts from the Ritual books and the Commentaries)

Translated by

Maurice Bloomfield

(Text in English)

Greenwood Press

New York

1969

O. I: The book belongs to the series 'The sacred books of East' volume 42. There are twenty four Roman Numbered preliminary pages followed by 716 textual pages numbered in Arabic numerals.

There are bibliographical footnotes.

Height: 23 cm.

B. T. P: ISBN – 0837118794 Accession no. -6251

MARC21: BIBLIOGRAPHIC FORMAT

LEADER (M):

n	a	m	a
Record Status	Type of record	Bibliographical level	Descriptive Catg.Form

CONTROL FIELD-MONOGRAPH & SERIAL (008)

t	1 9 6 9		n y u		g
Type of Date	Date1	Date2	Place of Publ.	Illustration	Target Audience

#						#	
Form Of Item	Nature of Contents	Govt. Pub.	Conf. Pub.	Festschrift	Index	Undefined	Literary Form

	e n g	#	
Biography	Language	Modified Record	Cata. Source

NAME OF THE FIELD INCL. MARC21 TAG	INDICATORS 1	2	DATA WITH SUBFIELD IDENTIFIERS
ISBN NO. (020) (R)	#	#	$a 0837118794 $c
ISSN (022) (R)	#	#	$a
DEWEY DECIMAL CLASSIFICATION NUMBER (082) (R)	0	#	$a $b
MAIN ENTRY-PERSONAL NAME (100) (NR)			$a 294.5 / 921.5 $b 20th ed $c
MAIN ENTRY –CORPORATE NAME (110) NR		#	$a $b $c $d $n
MAIN ENTRY – MEETING name (111) (NR)		#	$a $c $d $e $n
MAIN ENTRY - UNIFORM TITLE (130) (NR)		#	$a Vedas $d $k Atharva-veda $l English $n
TITLA STATEMENT (245) (NR)			$a Hymns of the Atharva-Veda $b together of the with extracts from the ritual books and the commentaries $c Translated by Maurice Bloomfield
EDITION STATEMENT (250) (nr)	#	#	$a $b

PUBLICATION DIST. ETC.(260) ®	3	#	$a New York $b Greenwood Press $c 1969
PHYSICAL DESC. (300) ®	#	#	$a xxiv, 716p. $b $c 23 cm. $e
SERIES STATEMENT/ ADDED ENTRY-TITLE (440) (R)	#		$a $n
SERIES STATEMENT (490) (R)		#	$a The Sacred books of the East ; v.42
GENERAL NOTE (500) (R)	#	#	$a Bibliographical footnotes
CONTENTS NOTE (505) (R)		#	$a
SUBJECT ADDED ENTRY-PERSONAL NAME (600) (R)		0	$a Bloomfield, Maurice $b $c
SUBJECT ADDED ENTRY-CORPORATE NAME (610) (R)		0	$a $c $d
SUBJECT ADDED ENTRY-TOPICAL NAME (650) (R)		0	$a $v $x $y $z
SUBJECT ADDED ENTRY-GEOGRAPHIC NAME (651) (R)	#	0	$a $v
ADDED ENTRY-PERSONAL NAME (700) (R)		#	$a $b $c
ADDED ENTRY-CORPORATE NAME (710) (R)		#	$a $b $c

			$d
ADDED ENTRY- MEETING NAME (711 (R)		#	$a $c $d
ADDED ENTRY – UNIFORM TITLE (730) (R)		#	$a
LOCATION (852)	1	#	$a
ACCESSION NO. INCL. DT. (901)			$a 31 $b 6-10-07 $c
CALL NO. (902)			$a 294.5 / 921.5 K69
SUBJECT HEADING DEFINED BY (903)			$a S.Das
ENTERED BY (904)			$a S.Das
VERIFIED BY (905)			$a S.Das

NB. #= Put blank. R means Repeatable. NR means Not Repeatable

EXAMPLE 32

The Recognition of Sakuntala of Kalidasa (a play in seven acts)

Translated with an Introduction and Notes

By

W. J. Johnson

Oxford University Press

New York

2001

O. I: - Test in English and Sanskrit .The book contains thirty-six preliminary pages in Roman numerals and 147 textual pages in Arabic numerals. It includes translated from Sanskrit and Bibliographical reference. "The Sakuntala in the Mahabharata (Mahabharata 1.62-9)"

B. T. P: - ISBN – 019283911X. Accession no. – 2704

MARC21: BIBLIOGRAPHIC FORMAT

LEADER (M):

Record Status	Type of record	Bibliographical level	Descriptive Catg.Form
n	a	m	a

CONTROL FIELD-MONOGRAPH & SERIAL (008)

Type of Date	Date1	Date2	Place of Publ.	Illustration	Target Audience
t	2 0 0 1		o x n		g

Form Of Item	Nature of Contents	Govt. Pub.	Conf. Pub.	Festschrift	Index	Undefined	Literary Form
#						#	

Biography	Language	Modified Record	Cata. Source
	e n g	#	

NAME OF THE FIELD INCL. MARC21 TAG	INDICATORS 1	2	DATA WITH SUBFIELD IDENTIFIERS
ISBN NO. (020) (R)	#	#	$a 19283911-X $c
ISSN (022) (R)	#	#	$a
DEWEY DECIMAL CLASSIFICATION NUMBER (082) (R)	0	#	$a 891.22 $b 20th ed
MAIN ENTRY-PERSONAL NAME (100) (NR)			$a $b $c
MAIN ENTRY – CORPORATE NAME (110) NR		#	$a $b $c $d $n
MAIN ENTRY – MEETING name (111) (NR)		#	$a $c $d $e $n
MAIN ENTRY - UNIFORM TITLE (130) (NR)		#	$a Kalidasa $d $k Sakuntala $l English. Sanskrit $n Selections
TITLA STATEMENT (245) (NR)			$a The recognition of Sakuntala of Kalidasa $b a play in seven acts $c translated with an introduction and notes by W.J. Johnson
EDITION STATEMENT (250) (nr)	#	#	$a $b
PUBLICATION DIST.	3	#	$a New York

ETC.(260) ®			$bOxford University Press $c 2001
PHYSICAL DESC. (300) ®	#	#	$a xxxvi, 147p. $b $c 20 cm. $e
SERIES STATEMENT/ ADDED ENTRY-TITLE (440) (R)	#		$a $n
SERIES STATEMENT (490) (R)		#	$a
GENERAL NOTE (500) (R)	#	#	$a "The Sakuntala in the Mahabharata (Mahabharata 1.62-9)". – includes bibliographical references. – includes translation from Sanskrit
CONTENTS NOTE (505) (R)		#	$a
SUBJECT ADDED ENTRY-PERSONAL NAME (600) (R)		0	$a $b $c
SUBJECT ADDED ENTRY-CORPORATE NAME (610) (R)		0	$a $c $d
SUBJECT ADDED ENTRY-TOPICAL NAME (650) (R)		0	$a $v $x $y $z
SUBJECT ADDED ENTRY-GEOGRAPHIC NAME (651) (R)	#	0	$a $v

3ADDED ENTRY- PERSONAL NAME (700) (R)		#	$a Johnson, W.J. $b $c
ADDED ENTRY- CORPORATE NAME (710) (R)		#	$a $b $c $d
ADDED ENTRY- MEETING NAME (711 (R)		#	$a $c $d
ADDED ENTRY – UNIFORM TITLE (730) (R)		#	$a
LOCATION (852)	1	#	$a
ACCESSION NO. INCL. DT. (901)			$a 32 $b 6-10-07 $c
CALL NO. (902)			$a 891.22 P01
SUBJECT HEADING DEFINED BY (903)			$a S.Das
ENTERED BY (904)			$a S.Das
VERIFIED BY (905)			$a S.Das

NB. #= Put blank. R means Repeatable. NR means Not Repeatable

EXAMPLE 33

The Agni PuranasTranslated and Annotated

by

N. Gangadharan

Motilal Banarsidass

Delhi

1984-1987

O. I: - Text in English.This Agni Puranas of four volumes is comprehensive in formation of more than one thousand Puranic themes of all important aspects of the Puranas. Height: 23 cm. The book belongs to 'Ancient Indian traditional & mythology, v.23-30.B. T. P: - ISBN- 0895817438. Accession no. - 4506.

MARC21: BIBLIOGRAPHIC FORMAT

LEADER (M):

Record Status	Type of record	Bibliographical level	Descriptive Catg.Form
n	a	m	a

CONTROL FIELD-MONOGRAPH & SERIAL (008)

Type of Date	Date1	Date2	Place of Publ.	Illustration	Target Audience
t	1 9 8 4	1 9 8 7	d e i		g

Form Of Item	Nature of Contents	Govt. Pub.	Conf. Pub.	Festschrift	Index	Undefined	Literary Form
#						#	

Biography	Language	Modified Record	Cata. Source
	e n g	#	

NAME OF THE FIELD INCL. MARC21 TAG	INDICATORS 1	2	DATA WITH SUBFIELD IDENTIFIERS
ISBN NO. (020) (R)	#	#	$a 0895817438 $c
ISSN (022) (R)	#	#	$a
DEWEY DECIMAL CLASSIFICATION NUMBER (082) (R)	0	#	$a 294.5/925 $b 20th ed
MAIN ENTRY-PERSONAL NAME (100) (NR)			$a $b $c
MAIN ENTRY –CORPORATE NAME (110) NR		#	$a $b $c $d $n
MAIN ENTRY – MEETING name (111) (NR)		#	$a $c $d $e $n
MAIN ENTRY - UNIFORM TITLE (130) (NR)		#	$a Puranas $d Agnipurana $k English $l $n
TITLA STATEMENT (245) (NR)			$a The Agni puranas $b translated and annotated by N. Gangadharan $c
EDITION STATEMENT (250) (nr)	#	#	$a $b
PUBLICATION DIST. ETC.(260) ®	3	#	$a Delhi $b Motilal Banaraidass

			$c 1984-1987
PHYSICAL DESC. (300) ®	#	#	$a 4v. $b $c 23 cm. $e
SERIES STATEMENT/ ADDED ENTRY-TITLE (440) (R)	#		$a $n
SERIES STATEMENT (490) (R)		#	$a Ancient Indian Tradition & Mythology ; v.27-30
GENERAL NOTE (500) (R)	#	#	$a
CONTENTS NOTE (505) (R)		#	$a
SUBJECT ADDED ENTRY- PERSONAL NAME (600) (R)		0	$a Gangadharan, N. $b $c
SUBJECT ADDED ENTRY- CORPORATE NAME (610) (R)		0	$a $c $d
SUBJECT ADDED ENTRY- TOPICAL NAME (650) (R)		0	$a $v $x $y $z
SUBJECT ADDED ENTRY- GEOGRAPHIC NAME (651) (R)	#	0	$a $v
ADDED ENTRY- PERSONAL NAME (700) (R)		#	$a $b $c
ADDED ENTRY- CORPORATE NAME (710) (R)		#	$a $b $c $d
ADDED ENTRY- MEETING		#	$a

NAME (711 (R)			$c $d
ADDED ENTRY – UNIFORM TITLE (730) (R)		#	$a
LOCATION (852)	1	#	$a
ACCESSION NO. INCL. DT. (901)			$a 33 $b 6-10-07 $c
CALL NO. (902)			$a 294.5/925 M84-87
SUBJECT HEADING DEFINED BY (903)			$a S.Das
ENTERED BY (904)			$a S. Das
VERIFIED BY (905)			$a S.Das

NB. #= Put blank. R means Repeatable. NR means Not Repeatable

7

MARC 21: Bibliographic Format of Multivolumed Books

EXAMPLE 34

College Botany

(In 2 Vol.)

H.C. Ganguly, Kumud Sankar Das, Chittatosh Dutta.

2nd edition.

Edited By

P.K Das.

New Central Book Agency Pvt. Ltd.

Kolkata.2005

O.I.- Height-26cm. ISBN- 81-73.81-028-1/ Price. 575.00(Set)/Vol1-Monocotyldons; Vol-2Angiosperms & Gymnosperms.It has a CD

MARC21: BIBLIOGRAPHIC FORMAT

LEADER (M):

n	a	m	a
Record Status	Type of record	Bibliographical level	Descriptive Catg.Form

CONTROL FIELD-MONOGRAPH & SERIAL (008)

t	2005		koi	a	g
Type of Date	Date1	Date2	Place of Publ.	Illustration	Target Audience

#						#	
Form Of Item	Nature of Contents	Govt. Pub.	Conf. Pub.	Festschrift	Index	Undefined	Literary Form

	eng	#	
Biography	Language	Modified Record	Cata. Source

NAME OF THE FIELD INCL. MARC21 TAG	INDICATORS 1	2	DATA WITH SUBFIELD IDENTIFIERS
ISBN NO. (020) (R)	#	#	$a 8173810281(pbk.) $c
ISSN (022) (R)	#	#	$a
DEWEY DECIMAL CLASSIFICATION NUMBER (082) (R)	0	#	$a 581 $b 20th ed
MAIN ENTRY-PERSONAL NAME (100) (NR)			$a Ganguly, H.C. $b $c
MAIN ENTRY – CORPORATE NAME (110) NR		#	$a $b $c $d $n
MAIN ENTRY – MEETING name (111) (NR)		#	$a $c $d $e $n
MAIN ENTRY - UNIFORM TITLE (130) (NR)		#	$a Ganguly, H.C. $d $k $l $n
TITLA STATEMENT (245) (NR)			$a College botany $b $cH.C. Ganguly, Kumud Sankar Das, Chittatosh Dutta
EDITION STATEMENT (250) (nr)	#	#	$a 2nd ed. edited by P.K.Das $b
PUBLICATION DIST.	3	#	$a Kolkata

ETC.(260) ®			$b New Central Book Agency $c 2005
PHYSICAL DESC. (300) ®	#	#	$a 2v. $b ill. $c 26 cm. + CD $e
SERIES STATEMENT/ ADDED ENTRY-TITLE (440) (R)	#		$a $n
SERIES STATEMENT (490) (R)		#	$a vol.1.Monocotyldons-vol.2. Angiosperms, Gymnosperm
GENERAL NOTE (500) (R)	#	#	$a
CONTENTS NOTE (505) (R)		#	$a
SUBJECT ADDED ENTRY-PERSONAL NAME (600) (R)		0	$a $b $c
SUBJECT ADDED ENTRY-CORPORATE NAME (610) (R)		0	$a $c $d
SUBJECT ADDED ENTRY-TOPICAL NAME (650) (R)		0	$a Botany $v $x $y $z
SUBJECT ADDED ENTRY-GEOGRAPHIC NAME (651) (R)	#	0	$a $v
ADDED ENTRY- PERSONAL NAME (700) (R)		#	$a $b $c
ADDED ENTRY- CORPORATE NAME (710) (R)		#	$a Das, Kumud Sankar, Dutta, Chittatos, Das,

			P.K. $b $c $d
ADDED ENTRY- MEETING NAME (711 (R)		#	$a $c $d
ADDED ENTRY – UNIFORM TITLE (730) (R)		#	$a
LOCATION (852)	1	#	$a
ACCESSION NO. INCL. DT. (901)			$a 34 $b 6-10-07 $c
CALL NO. (902)			$a 581 P 05
SUBJECT HEADING DEFINED BY (903)			$a S.Das
ENTERED BY (904)			$a S.Das
VERIFIED BY (905)			$a S.Das

NB. #= Put blank. R means Repeatable. NR means Not Repeatable

EXAMPLE 35

Dewey Decimal Classification and Relative Index

(4 VOL)

Deviced By

Melville Dewey

(Edition 20)

Edited By

John P. Comaromi

Forest Press

New York

1989

O.I.-Height-23cm. Vol. 1 – Introduction, Tables / Vol.2-3 – Schedules / Vol. 4- Relative index, manual

MARC21: BIBLIOGRAPHIC FORMAT

LEADER (M):

Record Status	Type of record	Bibliographical level	Descriptive Catg.Form
n	a	m	a

CONTROL FIELD-MONOGRAPH & SERIAL (008)

Type of Date	Date1				Date2				Place of Publ.			Illustration				Target Audience
t	1	9	8	4					n	y	u					g

Form Of Item	Nature of Contents				Govt. Pub.	Conf. Pub.	Festschrift	Index	Undefined	Literary Form
#									#	

Biography	Language			Modified Record	Cata. Source
	e	n	g	#	

NAME OF THE FIELD INCL. MARC21 TAG	INDICATORS 1	2	DATA WITH SUBFIELD IDENTIFIERS
ISBN NO. (020) (R)	#	#	$a 3468934109 $c 450.00
ISSN (022) (R)	#	#	$a
DEWEY DECIMAL CLASSIFICATION NUMBER (082) (R)	0	#	$a 025.431 $b 20th ed
MAIN ENTRY-PERSONAL NAME (100) (NR)			$a Dewey, Melville $b $c
MAIN ENTRY – CORPORATE NAME (110) NR		#	$a $b $c $d $n
MAIN ENTRY – MEETING name (111) (NR)		#	$a $c $d $e $n
MAIN ENTRY - UNIFORM TITLE (130) (NR)		#	$a $d $k $l $n
TITLA STATEMENT (245) (NR)			$a Dewey decimal classification and relative index $b $cdevised by Melville Dewey
EDITION STATEMENT (250) (nr)	#	#	$a 20th ed $b edited by John P. Comaromi

PUBLICATION DIST. ETC.(260) ®	3	#	$a New York $b Forest Press $c 1989
PHYSICAL DESC. (300) ®	#	#	$a 4v. $b $c 23 cm. $e
SERIES STATEMENT/ ADDED ENTRY-TITLE (440) (R)	#		$a $n
SERIES STATEMENT (490) (R)		#	$a
GENERAL NOTE (500) (R)	#	#	$a
CONTENTS NOTE (505) (R)		#	$a Vol.1 Introduction - V2-3 Schedule – V4 Relative index, Manual
SUBJECT ADDED ENTRY-PERSONAL NAME (600) (R)		0	$a $b $c
SUBJECT ADDED ENTRY-CORPORATE NAME (610) (R)		0	$a $c $d
SUBJECT ADDED ENTRY-TOPICAL NAME (650) (R)		0	$a Classification scheme, Dewey decimal $v $x $y $z
SUBJECT ADDED ENTRY-GEOGRAPHIC NAME (651) (R)	#	0	$a Library Classification $v
ADDED ENTRY-PERSONAL NAME (700) (R)		#	$a Comaromi, John, ed. $b $c
ADDED ENTRY-		#	$a

CORPORATE NAME (710) (R)			$b $c $d
ADDED ENTRY- MEETING NAME (711 (R)		#	$a $c $d
ADDED ENTRY – UNIFORM TITLE (730) (R)		#	$a
LOCATION (852)	1	#	$a
ACCESSION NO. INCL. DT. (901)			$a 35 $b 6-10-07 $c
CALL NO. (902)			$a 025.431 M 89
SUBJECT HEADING DEFINED BY (903)			$a S. Das
ENTERED BY (904)			$a S. Das
VERIFIED BY (905)			$a S.Das

NB. #= Put blank. R means Repeatable. NR means Not Repeatable

EXAMPLE 36

LAL'S Commentary on Water Pollution
with
Environment (protection) Laws
(2Vol)

M.C.Mehta

4th ed

Delhi Law House
Delhi

2007

O.I.- Height-26cm., Contains Bibliography(p967-p.989)/ ISBN- 81-86976-19- / Vol.2- Part-V-Ch VI to Appendix/ Price- 1095.00 per volume

MARC21: BIBLIOGRAPHIC FORMAT

LEADER (M):

Record Status	Type of record	Bibliographical level	Descriptive Catg.Form
n	a	m	a

CONTROL FIELD-MONOGRAPH & SERIAL (008)

Type of Date	Date1	Date2	Place of Publ.	Illustration	Target Audience
t	2 0 0 7		d e i		g

Form Of Item	Nature of Contents	Govt. Pub.	Conf. Pub.	Festschrift	Index	Undefined	Literary Form
#						#	

Biography	Language	Modified Record	Cata. Source
	e n g	#	

NAME OF THE FIELD INCL. MARC21 TAG	INDICATORS 1	2	DATA WITH SUBFIELD IDENTIFIERS
ISBN NO. (020) (R)	#	#	$a 8186976191 $c 1095.00
ISSN (022) (R)	#	#	$a
DEWEY DECIMAL CLASSIFICATION NUMBER (082) (R)	0	#	$a 344.046 $b 20th ed
MAIN ENTRY-PERSONAL NAME (100) (NR)			$a Mehta, M.C. $b $c
MAIN ENTRY –CORPORATE NAME (110) NR		#	$a $b $c $d $n
MAIN ENTRY – MEETING name (111) (NR)		#	$a $c $d $e $n
MAIN ENTRY - UNIFORM TITLE (130) (NR)		#	$a $d $k $l $n
TITLA STATEMENT (245) (NR)			$a Lal's Commentary on water pollution with environment (protection) laws $b $c M.C. Mehta
EDITION STATEMENT (250) (nr)	#	#	$a 4th ed $b
PUBLICATION DIST.	3	#	$a Delhi

ETC.(260) ®			$b Delhi Law House $c 2007
PHYSICAL DESC. (300) ®	#	#	$a 2v. $b $c 26 cm. $e
SERIES STATEMENT/ ADDED ENTRY-TITLE (440) (R)	#		$a $n
SERIES STATEMENT (490) (R)		#	$a
GENERAL NOTE (500) (R)	#	#	$a Along with Allied laws, states acts, Rules and notification. – Bibliography: p.967-989 (V.2)
CONTENTS NOTE (505) (R)		#	$a Vol.1 up to pt.IV-Vol.2 ptV to Appendix
SUBJECT ADDED ENTRY- PERSONAL NAME (600) (R)		0	$a $b $c
SUBJECT ADDED ENTRY- CORPORATE NAME (610) (R)		0	$a $c $d
SUBJECT ADDED ENTRY- TOPICAL NAME (650) (R)		0	$a Environment protection law, Water pollution $v $x $y $z
SUBJECT ADDED ENTRY- GEOGRAPHIC NAME (651) (R)	#	0	$a $v
ADDED ENTRY- PERSONAL NAME		#	$a $b

(700) (R)			$c
ADDED ENTRY- CORPORATE NAME (710) (R)		#	$a $b $c $d
ADDED ENTRY- MEETING NAME (711 (R)		#	$a $c $d
ADDED ENTRY – UNIFORM TITLE (730) (R)		#	$a
LOCATION (852)	1	#	$a
ACCESSION NO. INCL. DT. (901)			$a 36 $b 6-10-07 $c
CALL NO. (902)			$a 344.046 P 07
SUBJECT HEADING DEFINED BY (903)			$a S.Das
ENTERED BY (904)			$a S.Das
VERIFIED BY (905)			$a S.Das

NB. #= Put blank. R means Repeatable. NR means Not Repeatable

EXAMPLE 37

Studies in Botany
A Complete Textbook
for
Degree Course (B.Sc) Students

(2 vol)

Debabrata Mitra , Jibesh Guha, Salil Kr. Chowdhury

7th ed

Moulic Library

Kolkata

2002

O.I.-26c.m./vol1-Fungi.to Pteridophyta, vol2-Monocotyldons to appendix / Price. 225.00(per vol)/ ISBN- 81-2075-035-3

MARC21: BIBLIOGRAPHIC FORMAT

LEADER (M):

Record Status	Type of record	Bibliographical level	Descriptive Catg.Form
n	a	m	a

CONTROL FIELD-MONOGRAPH & SERIAL (008)

Type of Date	Date1	Date2	Place of Publ.	Illustration	Target Audience
t	2 0 0 2		k o i	a	g

Form Of Item	Nature of Contents	Govt. Pub.	Conf. Pub.	Festschrift	Index	Undefined	Literary Form
#						#	

Biography	Language	Modified Record	Cata. Source
	e n g	#	

NAME OF THE FIELD INCL. MARC21 TAG	INDICATORS 1	2	DATA WITH SUBFIELD IDENTIFIERS
ISBN NO. (020) (R)	#	#	$a 8120750353 $c 225.00
ISSN (022) (R)	#	#	$a
DEWEY DECIMAL CLASSIFICATION NUMBER (082) (R)	0	#	$a 581 $b 20th ed
MAIN ENTRY-PERSONAL NAME (100) (NR)			$a Mitra, Debabrata $b $c
MAIN ENTRY – CORPORATE NAME (110) NR		#	$a $b $c $d $n
MAIN ENTRY – MEETING name (111) (NR)		#	$a $c $d $e $n
MAIN ENTRY - UNIFORM TITLE (130) (NR)		#	$a $d $k $l $n
TITLA STATEMENT (245) (NR)			$a Studies in botany: $b complete textbook for degree course (B.Sc) students $c Debabrata Mitra, Jibesh Guha, Salil Kr. Chowdhury
EDITION STATEMENT (250) (nr)	#	#	$a 7th ed $b

PUBLICATION DIST. ETC.(260) ®	3	#	$a Kolkata $b Moulic Library $c 2002
PHYSICAL DESC. (300) ®	#	#	$a 2v. $b col. $c 26 cm. $e
SERIES STATEMENT/ ADDED ENTRY-TITLE (440) (R)	#		$a $n
SERIES STATEMENT (490) (R)		#	$a
GENERAL NOTE (500) (R)	#	#	$a Vol.1 Fungi. to Pteriophyta. – V. 2 Monocotydor to appendix
CONTENTS NOTE (505) (R)		#	$a
SUBJECT ADDED ENTRY-PERSONAL NAME (600) (R)		0	$a $b $c
SUBJECT ADDED ENTRY-CORPORATE NAME (610) (R)		0	$a $c $d
SUBJECT ADDED ENTRY-TOPICAL NAME (650) (R)		0	$a Botany $v $x $y $z
SUBJECT ADDED ENTRY-GEOGRAPHIC NAME (651) (R)	#	0	$a $v
ADDED ENTRY-PERSONAL NAME (700) (R)		#	$a Guha, Jibesh, $b Chowdhury, Salil Kr. $c
ADDED ENTRY-		#	$a

CORPORATE NAME (710) (R)			$b $c $d
ADDED ENTRY-MEETING NAME (711 (R)		#	$a $c $d
ADDED ENTRY – UNIFORM TITLE (730) (R)		#	$a
LOCATION (852)	1	#	$a
ACCESSION NO. INCL. DT. (901)			$a 37 $b 6-10-07 $c
CALL NO. (902)			$a 581 P02
SUBJECT HEADING DEFINED BY (903)			$a S.Das
ENTERED BY (904)			$a S.Das
VERIFIED BY (905)			$a S.Das

NB. #= Put blank. R means Repeatable. NR means Not Repeatable

EXAMPLE 38

Statistical Method
in
Commerce, Accountancy and Economics

(In 2 volumes)

N.G. Das.

N. Das and Co

Kolkata

1997

O.I.-23cm. / Price 160.00(Set).

MARC21: BIBLIOGRAPHIC FORMAT

LEADER (M):

Record Status	Type of record	Bibliographical level	Descriptive Catg.Form
n	a	m	a

CONTROL FIELD-MONOGRAPH & SERIAL (008)

Type of Date	Date1	Date2	Place of Publ.	Illustration	Target Audience
t	1 9 9 7		k o i		g

Form Of Item	Nature of Contents	Govt. Pub.	Conf. Pub.	Festschrift	Index	Undefined	Literary Form
#						#	

Biography	Language	Modified Record	Cata. Source
	e n g	#	

NAME OF THE FIELD INCL. MARC21 TAG	INDICATORS 1	2	DATA WITH SUBFIELD IDENTIFIERS
ISBN NO. (020) (R)	#	#	$a 815287974(pbk.) $c 160.00
ISSN (022) (R)	#	#	$a
DEWEY DECIMAL CLASSIFICATION NUMBER (082) (R)	0	#	$a 310 $b 20th ed
MAIN ENTRY-PERSONAL NAME (100) (NR)			$a Das, N.G. $b $c
MAIN ENTRY – CORPORATE NAME (110) NR		#	$a $b $c $d $n
MAIN ENTRY – MEETING name (111) (NR)		#	$a $c $d $e $n
MAIN ENTRY - UNIFORM TITLE (130) (NR)		#	$a $d $k $l $n
TITLA STATEMENT (245) (NR)			$a Statistical method in commerce, accountancy and economics $b $c N.G. Das
EDITION STATEMENT (250) (nr)	#	#	$a $b
PUBLICATION DIST. ETC.(260) ®	3	#	$a Kolkata $b N. Das and Co.

			$c 1997
PHYSICAL DESC. (300) ®	#	#	$a 2v $b $c 23 cm. $e
SERIES STATEMENT/ ADDED ENTRY-TITLE (440) (R)	#		$a $n
SERIES STATEMENT (490) (R)		#	$a
GENERAL NOTE (500) (R)	#	#	$a
CONTENTS NOTE (505) (R)		#	$a
SUBJECT ADDED ENTRY- PERSONAL NAME (600) (R)		0	$a $b $c
SUBJECT ADDED ENTRY- CORPORATE NAME (610) (R)		0	$a $c $d
SUBJECT ADDED ENTRY- TOPICAL NAME (650) (R)		0	$a Statistics, Accountancy, Economics $v $x $y $z
SUBJECT ADDED ENTRY- GEOGRAPHIC NAME (651) (R)	#	0	$a $v
ADDED ENTRY- PERSONAL NAME (700) (R)		#	$a $b $c
ADDED ENTRY- CORPORATE NAME		#	$a $b

(710) (R)			$c $d
ADDED ENTRY- MEETING NAME (711 (R)		#	$a $c $d
ADDED ENTRY – UNIFORM TITLE (730) (R)		#	$a
LOCATION (852)	1	#	$a
ACCESSION NO. INCL. DT. (901)			$a 38 $b 6-10-07 $c
CALL NO. (902)			$a 310 N 97
SUBJECT HEADING DEFINED BY (903)			$a S.Das
ENTERED BY (904)			$a S.Das
VERIFIED BY (905)			$a S.Das

NB. #= Put blank. R means Repeatable. NR means Not Repeatable

EXAMPLE 39

Avesta:The Sacred Books of Parsis

Edited By

Karl F. Geldner

(Text in English)

Indian edition

Parimal Publications

Delhi

1982

O.I. - The book is in 3 volumes. Height: 33cm. /B. T. P.:- Reprint. Originally published in Stuttgart by W. Kohlhammer on 1886./ISBN 978818420226. / Includes bibliographical references.

MARC21: BIBLIOGRAPHIC FORMAT

LEADER (M):

Record Status	Type of record	Bibliographical level	Descriptive Catg.Form
n	a	m	a

CONTROL FIELD-MONOGRAPH & SERIAL (008)

Type of Date	Date1	Date2	Place of Publ.	Illustration	Target Audience
t	1 9 8 2		d e i		g

Form Of Item	Nature of Contents	Govt. Pub.	Conf. Pub.	Festschrift	Index	Undefined	Literary Form
#						#	

Biography	Language	Modified Record	Cata. Source
	e n g	#	

NAME OF THE FIELD INCL. MARC21 TAG	INDICATORS 1	2	DATA WITH SUBFIELD IDENTIFIERS
ISBN NO. (020) (R)	#	#	$a 97881420226 $c
ISSN (022) (R)	#	#	$a
DEWEY DECIMAL CLASSIFICATION NUMBER (082) (R)	0	#	$a 290 $b 20th ed
MAIN ENTRY-PERSONAL NAME (100) (NR)			$a $b $c
MAIN ENTRY –CORPORATE NAME (110) NR		#	$a $b $c $d $n
MAIN ENTRY – MEETING name (111) (NR)		#	$a $c $d $e $n
MAIN ENTRY - UNIFORM TITLE (130) (NR)		#	$a $d $k $l $n
TITLA STATEMENT (245) (NR)			$a Avesta, the sacred books of Paris $b $c edited by Karl F. Geldner
EDITION STATEMENT (250) (nr)	#	#	$a $b
PUBLICATION DIST.	3	#	$a Delhi

ETC.(260) ®			$b Publications $c 1982
PHYSICAL DESC. (300) ®	#	#	$a 3v. $b $c 33 cm. $e
SERIES STATEMENT/ ADDED ENTRY-TITLE (440) (R)	#		$a $n
SERIES STATEMENT (490) (R)		#	$a
GENERAL NOTE (500) (R)	#	#	$a Reprint. Originally published: Stuttgart: W.Kohlhammer, 1886. – includes bibliographical references
CONTENTS NOTE (505) (R)		#	$a
SUBJECT ADDED ENTRY- PERSONAL NAME (600) (R)		0	$a $b $c
SUBJECT ADDED ENTRY- CORPORATE NAME (610) (R)		0	$a $c $d
SUBJECT ADDED ENTRY- TOPICAL NAME (650) (R)		0	$a Sacred books $v $x $y $z
SUBJECT ADDED ENTRY- GEOGRAPHIC NAME (651) (R)	#	0	$a $v
ADDED ENTRY- PERSONAL NAME (700) (R)		#	$a Geldner, Karl R. $b $c

ADDED ENTRY- CORPORATE NAME (710) (R)		#	$a $b $c $d
ADDED ENTRY- MEETING NAME (711 (R)		#	$a $c $d
ADDED ENTRY – UNIFORM TITLE (730) (R)		#	$a
LOCATION (852)	1	#	$a
ACCESSION NO. INCL. DT. (901)			$a 39 $b 6-10-07 $c
CALL NO. (902)			$a 290 M82
SUBJECT HEADING DEFINED BY (903)			$a S.Das
ENTERED BY (904)			$a S.Das
VERIFIED BY (905)			$a S.Das

NB. #= Put blank. R means Repeatable. NR means Not Repeatable

EXAMPLE 40

Chhandogya Upanishad
with the commentary
of
Sri Madhvacharya,

(called also Anandatirtha)

Translated By
Srisa Chandra Vasu

(Text in English & Sanskrit)

AMS Press
New York

1974.

O.I. –There are fifteen Roman numbered preliminary pages followed by five hundred ninety one textual pages numbered in Arabic numerals. / Heigh - 23cm. / ISBN 9788284120216.

MARC21: BIBLIOGRAPHIC FORMAT

LEADER (M):

n	a	m	a
Record Status	Type of record	Bibliographical level	Descriptive Catg.Form

CONTROL FIELD-MONOGRAPH & SERIAL (008)

t	1974		nyu		g
Type of Date	Date1	Date2	Place of Publ.	Illustration	Target Audience

#						#	
Form Of Item	Nature of Contents	Govt. Pub.	Conf. Pub.	Festschrift	Index	Undefined	Literary Form

	eng	#	
Biography	Language	Modified Record	Cata. Source

NAME OF THE FIELD INCL. MARC21 TAG	INDICATORS 1	2	DATA WITH SUBFIELD IDENTIFIERS
ISBN NO. (020) (R)	#	#	$a 9788284120216 $c
ISSN (022) (R)	#	#	$a
DEWEY DECIMAL CLASSIFICATION NUMBER (082) (R)	0	#	$a 291.5 $b 20th ed
MAIN ENTRY-PERSONAL NAME (100) (NR)			$a $b $c
MAIN ENTRY – CORPORATE NAME (110) NR		#	$a $b $c $d $n
MAIN ENTRY – MEETING NAME (111) (NR)		#	$a $c $d $e $n
MAIN ENTRY - UNIFORM TITLE (130) (NR)		#	$a Upanishad $d $k $l English & Sanskrit $n
TITLA STATEMENT (245) (NR)			$a Chhandogya Upanishad $b $c with the commentary of Sri Mhadvacharaya, called also Anandatirtha ; translated by Srisa Chandra Vasu
EDITION STATEMENT (250) (nr)	#	#	$a $b

PUBLICATION DIST. ETC.(260) ®	3	#	$a New York $b AMS Press $c 1974
PHYSICAL DESC. (300) ®	#	#	$a xv, 591p. $b other physical details $c 23 cm. $e
SERIES STATEMENT/ ADDED ENTRY-TITLE (440) (R)	#		$a $n
SERIES STATEMENT (490) (R)		#	$a
GENERAL NOTE (500) (R)	#	#	$a English & Sanskrit: commentary in English
CONTENTS NOTE (505) (R)		#	$a
SUBJECT ADDED ENTRY- PERSONAL NAME (600) (R)		0	$a Vasu, Srisa Chandra $b $c
SUBJECT ADDED ENTRY- CORPORATE NAME (610) (R)		0	$a $c $d
SUBJECT ADDED ENTRY- TOPICAL NAME (650) (R)		0	$a $v $x $y $z
SUBJECT ADDED ENTRY- GEOGRAPHIC NAME (651) (R)	#	0	$a $v
ADDED ENTRY- PERSONAL NAME (700) (R)		#	$a $b $c
ADDED ENTRY- CORPORATE NAME (710) (R)		#	$a $b

			$c $d
ADDED ENTRY- MEETING NAME (711 (R)		#	$a $c $d
ADDED ENTRY – UNIFORM TITLE (730) (R)		#	$a
LOCATION (852)	1	#	$a
ACCESSION NO. INCL. DT. (901)			$a 40 $b 6-10-07 $c
CALL NO. (902)			$a 291.5 L74
SUBJECT HEADING DEFINED BY (903)			$a S.Das
ENTERED BY (904)			$a S.Das
VERIFIED BY (905)			$a S.Das

NB. #= Put blank. R means Repeatable. NR means Not Repeatable

EXAMPLE 41

The Kausitaki Upanisat

Translated

By

Srisa Chandra Vidyarnava and Mohan Lal Sandal.

(Text in English & Sanskrit)

Panini Office

Allahabad

1925

O.I. - There are twelve Roman numbered preliminary pages followed by five hundred sixteen textual pages numbered in Arabic numerals. Height: 24cm. It includes Sankarananda's commentary, the Kusitakibrahmanopanisddipika in English.

B. T. P.:- 08-3711879-5

MARC21: BIBLIOGRAPHIC FORMAT

LEADER (M):

Record Status	Type of record	Bibliographical level	Descriptive Catg.Form
n	a	m	a

CONTROL FIELD-MONOGRAPH & SERIAL (008)

Type of Date	Date1	Date2	Place of Publ.	Illustration	Target Audience
t	1 9 2 5		a l i		g

Form Of Item	Nature of Contents	Govt. Pub.	Conf. Pub.	Festschrift	Index	Undefined	Literary Form
#						#	

Biography	Language	Modified Record	Cata. Source
	e n g	#	

NAME OF THE FIELD INCL. MARC21 TAG	INDICATORS 1	2	DATA WITH SUBFIELD IDENTIFIERS
ISBN NO. (020) (R)	#	#	$a 0837118795 $c
ISSN (022) (R)	#	#	$a
DEWEY DECIMAL CLASSIFICATION NUMBER (082) (R)	0	#	$a 294.5 $b 20th ed
MAIN ENTRY-PERSONAL NAME (100) (NR)			$a $b $c
MAIN ENTRY –CORPORATE NAME (110) NR		#	$a $b $c $d $n
MAIN ENTRY – MEETING name (111) (NR)		#	$a $c $d $e $n
MAIN ENTRY - UNIFORM TITLE (130) (NR)		#	$a Upanishad $d $k $l English & Sanskrit $n
TITLA STATEMENT (245) (NR)			$a $b $c
EDITION STATEMENT (250) (nr)	#	#	$a $b
PUBLICATION DIST. ETC.(260) ®	3	#	$a Allahabad $b Panini Office $c 1925

PHYSICAL DESC. (300) ®	#	#	$a xii, 516p. $b $c 24 cm. $e
SERIES STATEMENT/ ADDED ENTRY-TITLE (440) (R)	#		$a $n
SERIES STATEMENT (490) (R)		#	$a
GENERAL NOTE (500) (R)	#	#	$a Includes Sankarananda's commentary, the Kusitaki brahmanopanisddipika in English
CONTENTS NOTE (505) (R)		#	$a
SUBJECT ADDED ENTRY- PERSONAL NAME (600) (R)		0	$a Vasu, Srisa Chandra, Sandal, Mohan Lal, Sankarananda $b $c
SUBJECT ADDED ENTRY- CORPORATE NAME (610) (R)		0	$a Upanishad $c $d
SUBJECT ADDED ENTRY- TOPICAL NAME (650) (R)		0	$a $v $x $y $z
SUBJECT ADDED ENTRY- GEOGRAPHIC NAME (651) (R)	#	0	$a $v
ADDED ENTRY- PERSONAL NAME (700) (R)		#	$a $b $c

ADDED ENTRY- CORPORATE NAME (710) (R)		#	$a $b $c $d
ADDED ENTRY- MEETING NAME (711 (R)		#	$a $c $d
ADDED ENTRY – UNIFORM TITLE (730) (R)		#	$a
LOCATION (852)	1	#	$a
ACCESSION NO. INCL. DT. (901)			$a 41 $b 6-10-07 $c
CALL NO. (902)			$a 294.5 F25
SUBJECT HEADING DEFINED BY (903)			$a S.Das
ENTERED BY (904)			$a S.Das
VERIFIED BY (905)			$a S.Das

NB. #= Put blank. R means Repeatable. NR means Not Repeatable

8

MARC 21: Bibliographic Format of Anonymous Books

EXAMPLE 42

Blessed Mother Goose
Nursery Rhymes
for
Today's Children

2nd edition

Compiled By
Frank Scully

Illustrated By
Keye Luke

House-Warven
California

1951

O.I.: 104p. with illustration. Size: 28cm

MARC21: BIBLIOGRAPHIC FORMAT

LEADER (M):

Record Status	Type of record	Bibliographical level	Descriptive Catg.Form
n	a	m	a

CONTROL FIELD-MONOGRAPH & SERIAL (008)

Type of Date	Date1	Date2	Place of Publ.	Illustration	Target Audience
t	1 9 5 1		c a #	a	g

Form Of Item	Nature of Contents	Govt. Pub.	Conf. Pub.	Festschrift	Index	Undefined	Literary Form
#						#	

Biography	Language	Modified Record	Cata. Source
	e n g	#	

NAME OF THE FIELD INCL. MARC21 TAG	INDICATORS 1	2	DATA WITH SUBFIELD IDENTIFIERS
ISBN NO. (020) (R)	#	#	$a 9782350016 $c 125.00
ISSN (022) (R)	#	#	$a
DEWEY DECIMAL CLASSIFICATION NUMBER (082) (R)	0	#	$a 398.8 $b 20th ed
MAIN ENTRY-PERSONAL NAME (100) (NR)			$a $b $c
MAIN ENTRY – CORPORATE NAME (110) NR		#	$a $b $c $d $n
MAIN ENTRY – MEETING name (111) (NR)		#	$a $c $d $e $n
MAIN ENTRY - UNIFORM TITLE (130) (NR)		#	$a Mother goose $d $k $l $n
TITLA STATEMENT (245) (NR)			$a Blessed mother goose $b nursery rhymes for today's children$c compiled by Frank Scully; illustrated by Keya Luke
EDITION STATEMENT (250) (nr)	#	#	$a 2nd ed $b

PUBLICATION DIST. ETC.(260) ®	3	#	$a California $b House-Warven $c 1951
PHYSICAL DESC. (300) ®	#	#	$a 104 p. $b illus. $c 28 cm. $e
SERIES STATEMENT/ ADDED ENTRY-TITLE (440) (R)	#		$a $n
SERIES STATEMENT (490) (R)		#	$a
GENERA NOTE (500) (R)	#	#	$a A collection of nursery rhymes
CONTENTS NOTE (505) (R)		#	$a
SUBJECT ADDED ENTRY-PERSONAL NAME (600) (R)		0	$a $b $c
SUBJECT ADDED ENTRY-CORPORATE NAME (610) (R)		0	$a $c $d
SUBJECT ADDED ENTRY-TOPICAL NAME (650) (R)	#	0	$a Music Rymes-Collections $v $x $y $z
SUBJECT ADDED ENTRY-GEOGRAPHIC NAME (651) (R)	#	0	$a $v
ADDED ENTRY-PERSONAL NAME (700) (R)	1	#	$a Scully, Frank, <u>comp.</u> $b $c
ADDED ENTRY-		#	$a

CORPORATE NAME (710) (R)			$b $c $d
ADDED ENTRY- MEETING NAME (711 (R)		#	$a $c $d
ADDED ENTRY – UNIFORM TITLE (730) (R)		#	$a
LOCATION (852)	1	#	$a
ACCESSION NO. INCL. DT. (901)			$a 42 $b 01-01-2005 $c
CALL NO. (902)			$a 398.8J51
SUBJECT HEADING DEFINED BY (903)			$a S.Das
ENTERED BY (904)			$a S.Das
VERIFIED BY (905)			$a S.Das

NB. #= Put blank. R means Repeatable. NR means Not Repeatable

EXAMPLE 43

Aladin and other Tales from Arabian Nights
(unknown)

Illustrated by

W. Heath Robinson and others

A. A. Knoppy..

New York

© 1993

O.l. 346p. With illustration. Size: 21cmISBN: 0679425330
Series: Everyman's library children's classics

MARC21: BIBLIOGRAPHIC FORMAT

LEADER (M):

Record Status	Type of record	Bibliographical level	Descriptive Catg.Form
a	n	m	a

CONTROL FIELD-MONOGRAPH & SERIAL (008)

Type of Date	Date1	Date2	Place of Publ.	Illustration	Target Audience
t	1 9 9 3		n y u	a	g

Form Of Item	Nature of Contents	Govt. Pub.	Conf. Pub.	Festschrift	Index	Undefined	Literary Form
#						#	

Biography	Language	Modified Record	Cata. Source
	e n g	#	

NAME OF THE FIELD INCL. MARC21 TAG	INDICATORS 1	2	DATA WITH SUBFIELD IDENTIFIERS
ISBN NO. (020) (R)	#	#	$a 0679425330 $c 478.00
ISSN (022) (R)	#	#	$a
DEWEY DECIMAL CLASSIFICATION NUMBER (082) (R)	0	#	$a 398.22 $b 20th ed
MAIN ENTRY-PERSONAL NAME (100) (NR)			$a $b $c
MAIN ENTRY – CORPORATE NAME (110) NR		#	$a $b $c $d $n
MAIN ENTRY – MEETING name (111) (NR)		#	$a $c $d $e $n
MAIN ENTRY - UNIFORM TITLE (130) (NR)		#	$a Arabian Night $d $k $l $n
TITLA STATEMENT (245) (NR)			$a Aladin and other tale from the Arabian night $b $c unknown; illustrated by W. Health Robinson and others
EDITION STATEMENT (250) (nr)	#	#	$a $b

PUBLICATION DIST. ETC.(260) ®	3	#	$a New York $b A.A. Knoppy $c 1993
PHYSICAL DESC. (300) ®	#	#	$a 346p. $b ill. $c 21 cm. $e
SERIES STATEMENT/ ADDED ENTRY-TITLE (440) (R)	#		$a Everyman's Library Children's Classics $n
SERIES STATEMENT (490) (R)		#	$a
GENERAL NOTE (500) (R)	#	#	$a A collection of tales told by seharazada to amuse the cruel Sultan and stop him from executing her as he ha killed his other daily wives
CONTENTS NOTE (505) (R)		#	$a
SUBJECT ADDED ENTRY- PERSONAL NAME (600) (R)		0	$a $b $c
SUBJECT ADDED ENTRY- CORPORATE NAME (610) (R)		0	$a $c $d
SUBJECT ADDED ENTRY- TOPICAL NAME (650) (R)		0	$a Arabs, $a Folklore $v $x Folklore $y $z Arab countries
SUBJECT ADDED ENTRY- GEOGRAPHIC NAME (651) (R)	#	0	$a $v
ADDED ENTRY- PERSONAL	1	#	$a Robinson, W. Health

NAME (700) (R)			$b $c
ADDED ENTRY- CORPORATE NAME (710) (R)		#	$a $b $c $d
ADDED ENTRY- MEETING NAME (711 (R)		#	$a $c $d
ADDED ENTRY – UNIFORM TITLE (730) (R)		#	$a
LOCATION (852)	1	#	$a
ACCESSION NO. INCL. DT. (901)			$a 43 $b 01-01-05 $c
CALL NO. (902)			$a 398.22N93
SUBJECT HEADING DEFINED BY (903)			$a S.Das
ENTERED BY (904)			$a S.Das
VERIFIED BY (905)			$a S.Das

NB. #= Put blank. R means Repeatable. NR means Not Repeatable

EXAMPLE 43

Ethics in African Dress: Children's stories

Compiled By

Zainabu Renner

Pine Hill Press

New York

1996

O.I.: 45p./ Size: 22cm / The book contains biographies of authors /ISBN: 1575790386

MARC21: BIBLIOGRAPHIC FORMAT

LEADER (M):

n	a	m	a
Record Status	Type of record	Bibliographical level	Descriptive Catg.Form

CONTROL FIELD-MONOGRAPH & SERIAL (008)

t	1 9 9 6		n y u		g
Type of Date	Date1	Date2	Place of Publ.	Illustration	Target Audience

#						#	
Form Of Item	Nature of Contents	Govt. Pub.	Conf. Pub.	Festschrift	Index	Undefined	Literary Form

	e n g	#	
Biography	Language	Modified Record	Cata. Source

NAME OF THE FIELD INCL. MARC21 TAG	INDICATORS 1	2	DATA WITH SUBFIELD IDENTIFIERS
ISBN NO. (020) (R)	#	#	$a 1575793086 $c 358.00
ISSN (022) (R)	#	#	$a
DEWEY DECIMAL CLASSIFICATION NUMBER (082) (R)	0	#	$a 398.2 $b 20th ed
MAIN ENTRY-PERSONAL NAME (100) (NR)			$a $b $c
MAIN ENTRY –CORPORATE NAME (110) NR		#	$a $b $c $d $n
MAIN ENTRY – MEETING name (111) (NR)		#	$a $c $d $e $n
MAIN ENTRY - UNIFORM TITLE (130) (NR)		#	$a Ethics an African dress $d $k $l $n
TITLA STATEMENT (245) (NR)			$a Ethics an African dress: $b Children's stories $c compiled by Zainabu Renner
EDITION STATEMENT (250) (nr)	#	#	$a $b
PUBLICATION DIST.	3	#	$a New York

ETC.(260) ®			$b Pinehill Press $c 1996
PHYSICAL DESC. (300) ®	#	#	$a 45p. $b $c 22 cm. $e
SERIES STATEMENT/ ADDED ENTRY-TITLE (440) (R)	#		$a $n
SERIES STATEMENT (490) (R)		#	$a
GENERAL NOTE (500) (R)	#	#	$a Includes biographies of authors. – A compilation of children short stories from Africa
CONTENTS NOTE (505) (R)		#	$a
SUBJECT ADDED ENTRY- PERSONAL NAME (600) (R)		0	$a $b $c
SUBJECT ADDED ENTRY- CORPORATE NAME (610) (R)		0	$a $c $d
SUBJECT ADDED ENTRY- TOPICAL NAME (650) (R)		0	$a A fables, African $a Fables $v $x $y $z
SUBJECT ADDED ENTRY- GEOGRAPHIC NAME (651) (R)	#	0	$a $v
ADDED ENTRY- PERSONAL NAME (700) (R)	1	#	$a Renner, Zainabu, comp. $b $c

ADDED ENTRY- CORPORATE NAME (710) (R)		#	$a $b $c $d
ADDED ENTRY- MEETING NAME (711 (R)		#	$a $c $d
ADDED ENTRY – UNIFORM TITLE (730) (R)		#	$a
LOCATION (852)	1	#	$a
ACCESSION NO. INCL. DT. (901)			$a 44 $b 01-01-05 $c
CALL NO. (902)			$a 398.2 N96
SUBJECT HEADING DEFINED BY (903)			$a S.Das
ENTERED BY (904)			$a S.Das
VERIFIED BY (905)			$a S.Das

NB. #= Put blank. R means Repeatable. NR means Not Repeatable

EXAMPLE 44

Indian Idylls
from
the Sanskrit of the
Mahabharata

(4th edition)

Edited by
Sir Edwin Arnold

Trubner and Co

London.

1883

O.I.: XII.21.282 p./ Size: 22cm

MARC21: BIBLIOGRAPHIC FORMAT

LEADER (M):

Record Status	Type of record	Bibliographical level	Descriptive Catg.Form
n	a	m	a

CONTROL FIELD-MONOGRAPH & SERIAL (008)

Type of Date	Date1	Date2	Place of Publ.	Illustration	Target Audience
t	1 8 8 3		1 o #		g

Form Of Item	Nature of Contents	Govt. Pub.	Conf. Pub.	Festschrift	Index	Undefined	Literary Form
#						#	

Biography	Language	Modified Record	Cata. Source
	e n g	#	

NAME OF THE FIELD INCL. MARC21 TAG	INDICATORS 1	2	DATA WITH SUBFIELD IDENTIFIERS
ISBN NO. (020) (R)	#	#	$a 0816557452 $c 395.00
ISSN (022) (R)	#	#	$a
DEWEY DECIMAL CLASSIFICATION NUMBER (082) (R)	0	#	$a 401.213 $b
MAIN ENTRY-PERSONAL NAME (100) (NR)			$a $b $c
MAIN ENTRY –CORPORATE NAME (110) NR		#	$a $b $c $d $n
MAIN ENTRY – MEETING name (111) (NR)		#	$a $c $d $e $n
MAIN ENTRY - UNIFORM TITLE (130) (NR)		#	$a Mahabharata $d $k $l $n
TITLA STATEMENT (245) (NR)			$a Indian idylls from the Sanskrit of the Mahabharata $b $c edited by Sir Edwin Arnold
EDITION STATEMENT (250) (nr)	#	#	$a 4th ed $b

PUBLICATION DIST. ETC.(260) ®	3	#	$a London $b Trubner $c 1883
PHYSICAL DESC. (300) ®	#	#	$a xii, 21, 282p. $b $c 22 cm. $e
SERIES STATEMENT/ ADDED ENTRY-TITLE (440) (R)	#		$a $n
SERIES STATEMENT (490) (R)		#	$a
GENERAL NOTE (500) (R)	#	#	$a Famous Hindu mythology about the royal conflict between Pandavas and Kouravas
CONTENTS NOTE (505) (R)		#	$a
SUBJECT ADDED ENTRY-PERSONAL NAME (600) (R)		0	$a $b $c
SUBJECT ADDED ENTRY-CORPORATE NAME (610) (R)		0	$a $c $d
SUBJECT ADDED ENTRY-TOPICAL NAME (650) (R)		0	$a Indian idylls $v $x $y $z
SUBJECT ADDED ENTRY-GEOGRAPHIC NAME (651) (R)	#	0	$a $v
ADDED ENTRY- PERSONAL NAME (700) (R)	1	#	$a Arnold, Edwin, ed. $b $c Sir
ADDED ENTRY- CORPORATE NAME (710) (R)		#	$a $b

			$c $d
ADDED ENTRY- MEETING NAME (711 (R)		#	$a $c $d
ADDED ENTRY – UNIFORM TITLE (730) (R)		#	$a
LOCATION (852)	1	#	$a
ACCESSION NO. INCL. DT. (901)			$a 45 $b 01-01-05 $c
CALL NO. (902)			$a 401.203 B88
SUBJECT HEADING DEFINED BY (903)			$a S.Das
ENTERED BY (904)			$a S.Das
VERIFIED BY (905)			$a S.Das

NB. #= Put blank. R means Repeatable. NR means Not Repeatable

EXAMPLE 45

Gita

English translations along with original shlokas

Saze Publication
Kolkata.

1990

O.I.: 120p. Size: 19cm

MARC21: BIBLIOGRAPHIC FORMAT

LEADER (M):

Record Status	Type of record	Bibliographical level	Descriptive Catg.Form
n	a	m	a

CONTROL FIELD-MONOGRAPH & SERIAL (008)

Type of Date	Date1	Date2	Place of Publ.	Illustration	Target Audience
t	1 9 9 0		k o i		g

Form Of Item	Nature of Contents	Govt. Pub.	Conf. Pub.	Festschrift	Index	Undefined	Literary Form
#						#	

Biography	Language	Modified Record	Cata. Source
	e n g	#	

NAME OF THE FIELD INCL. MARC21 TAG	INDICATORS 1	2	DATA WITH SUBFIELD IDENTIFIERS
ISBN NO. (020) (R)	#	#	$a 8166890013 $c 93.50
ISSN (022) (R)	#	#	$a
DEWEY DECIMAL CLASSIFICATION NUMBER (082) (R)	0	#	$a 294.5 $b 20th ed
MAIN ENTRY-PERSONAL NAME (100) (NR)			$a $b $c
MAIN ENTRY –CORPORATE NAME (110) NR		#	$a $b $c $d $n
MAIN ENTRY – MEETING name (111) (NR)		#	$a $c $d $e $n
MAIN ENTRY - UNIFORM TITLE (130) (NR)		#	$a Bhagawadgita $d $k $l $n
TITLA STATEMENT (245) (NR)			$a Gita $b $c
EDITION STATEMENT (250) (nr)	#	#	$a $b
PUBLICATION DIST. ETC.(260) ®	3	#	$a Kolkata $b Saze $c 1990

PHYSICAL DESC. (300) ®	#	#	$a 120p. $b $c 19 cm $e
SERIES STATEMENT/ ADDED ENTRY-TITLE (440) (R)	#		$a $n
SERIES STATEMENT (490) (R)		#	$a
GENERAL NOTE (500) (R)	#	#	$a Includes English translations along with original shlokas. – A famous holy book of Hinduism consists of shlokas delivered by Lord Shri Krishna to Arjuna during Kurukshetra war
CONTENTS NOTE (505) (R)		#	$a
SUBJECT ADDED ENTRY-PERSONAL NAME (600) (R)		0	$a $b $c
SUBJECT ADDED ENTRY-CORPORATE NAME (610) (R)		0	$a $c $d
SUBJECT ADDED ENTRY-TOPICAL NAME (650) (R)	#	0	$a Gita $v $x $y $z
SUBJECT ADDED ENTRY-GEOGRAPHIC NAME (651) (R)		0	$a $v
ADDED ENTRY-PERSONAL NAME (700) (R)		#	$a $b $c

ADDED ENTRY- CORPORATE NAME (710) (R)		#	$a $b $c $d
ADDED ENTRY- MEETING NAME (711 (R)		#	$a $c $d
ADDED ENTRY – UNIFORM TITLE (730) (R)		#	$a
LOCATION (852)	1	#	$a
ACCESSION NO. INCL. DT. (901)			$a 46 $b 01-01-05 $c
CALL NO. (902)			$a 294.5 N90
SUBJECT HEADING DEFINED BY (903)			$a S.Das
ENTERED BY (904)			$a S.Das
VERIFIED BY (905)			$a S.Das

NB. #= Put blank. R means Repeatable. NR means Not Repeatable

9

MARC 21: Bibliographic Format of Pseudoname

EXAMPLE 45

MIDDLE MARCH

George Eliot

(pseudo)

Edited with Notes
By
David Carool

with an
Introduction By
Felicia Bonaparte

Oxford University Press
Oxford

1998

O.I - Description : xivi, 810 page, ISBN- 0 -19 -283402,
Series-Oxford World's Classics,
Subject - English

MARC21: BIBLIOGRAPHIC FORMAT

LEADER (M):

Record Status	Type of record	Bibliographical level	Descriptive Catg.Form
n	a	m	a

CONTROL FIELD-MONOGRAPH & SERIAL (008)

Type of Date	Date1	Date2	Place of Publ.	Illustration	Target Audience
t	1 9 9 8		o x #		g

Form Of Item	Nature of Contents	Govt. Pub.	Conf. Pub.	Festschrift	Index	Undefined	Literary Form
#						#	

Biography	Language	Modified Record	Cata. Source
	e n g	#	

NAME OF THE FIELD INCL. MARC21 TAG	INDICATORS 1	2	DATA WITH SUBFIELD IDENTIFIERS
ISBN NO. (020) (R)	#	#	$a 019283402 $c 115.00
ISSN (022) (R)	#	#	$a
DEWEY DECIMAL CLASSIFICATION NUMBER (082) (R)	0	#	$a 823 $b 20th ed
MAIN ENTRY-PERSONAL NAME (100) (NR)	1		$a Eliot, George, pseudo. $b $c
MAIN ENTRY –CORPORATE NAME (110) NR		#	$a $b $c $d $n
MAIN ENTRY – MEETING name (111) (NR)		#	$a $c $d $e $n
MAIN ENTRY - UNIFORM TITLE (130) (NR)		#	$a $d $k $l $n
TITLA STATEMENT (245) (NR)			$a Middlemarch $b $c George Eliot ; edited with notes by David Carool
EDITION STATEMENT (250) (nr)	#	#	$a $b
PUBLICATION DIST.	3	#	$a Oxford

ETC.(260) ®			$b Oxford University Press $c 1998
PHYSICAL DESC. (300) ®	#	#	$a xivi, 810p. $b $c $e
SERIES STATEMENT/ ADDED ENTRY-TITLE (440) (R)	#		$a Oxford World's Classics $n
SERIES STATEMENT (490) (R)		#	$a
GENERAL NOTE (500) (R)	#	#	$a with an introduction by Felicia Bonaparte
CONTENTS NOTE (505) (R)		#	$a
SUBJECT ADDED ENTRY-PERSONAL NAME (600) (R)		0	$a $b $c
SUBJECT ADDED ENTRY-CORPORATE NAME (610) (R)		0	$a $c $d
SUBJECT ADDED ENTRY-TOPICAL NAME (650) (R)	#	0	$a English Fiction $v $x $y $z
SUBJECT ADDED ENTRY-GEOGRAPHIC NAME (651) (R)		0	$a $v
ADDED ENTRY- PERSONAL NAME (700) (R)	1	#	$a Carool, David, ed. $b $c
ADDED ENTRY- CORPORATE NAME (710) (R)		#	$a $b $c

			$d
ADDED ENTRY- MEETING NAME (711 (R)		#	$a $c $d
ADDED ENTRY – UNIFORM TITLE (730) (R)		#	$a
LOCATION (852)	1	#	$a
ACCESSION NO. INCL. DT. (901)			$a 47 $b 01-01-2005 $c
CALL NO. (902)			$a 823 N98
SUBJECT HEADING DEFINED BY (903)			$a S.Das
ENTERED BY (904)			$a S.Das
VERIFIED BY (905)			$a S.Das

NB. #= Put blank. R means Repeatable. NR means Not Repeatable

EXAMPLE 46

HOMAGE

To

Catalonia and Looking Back On The Spanish War

G. Orwell

(pseudo)

1977

O.I - Description - 246 page / Subject-English; Spanish war

MARC21: BIBLIOGRAPHIC FORMAT

LEADER (M):

Record Status	Type of record	Bibliographical level	Descriptive Catg.Form
n	a	m	a

....

CONTROL FIELD-MONOGRAPH & SERIAL (008)

Type of Date	Date1	Date2	Place of Publ.	Illustration	Target Audience
t	1977		###		g

Form Of Item	Nature of Contents	Govt. Pub.	Conf. Pub.	Festschrift	Index	Undefined	Literary Form
#						#	

Biography	Language	Modified Record	Cata. Source
	eng	#	

....

NAME OF THE FIELD INCL. MARC21 TAG	INDICATORS 1	2	DATA WITH SUBFIELD IDENTIFIERS
ISBN NO. (020) (R)	#	#	$a 0118955321 $c 245.00
ISSN (022) (R)	#	#	$a
DEWEY DECIMAL CLASSIFICATION NUMBER (082) (R)	0	#	$a 940.2526 $b 20th ed
MAIN ENTRY-PERSONAL NAME (100) (NR)	1		$a Orwell, G. pseud. $b $c
MAIN ENTRY – CORPORATE NAME (110) NR		#	$a $b $c $d $n
MAIN ENTRY – MEETING name (111) (NR)		#	$a $c $d $e $n
MAIN ENTRY - UNIFORM TITLE (130) (NR)		#	$a $d $k $l $n
TITLA STATEMENT (245) (NR)			$a Homage to catalonia an looking back on the Spanish war $b $c G. Orwell
EDITION STATEMENT (250) (nr)	#	#	$a $b
PUBLICATION DIST. ETC.(260) ®	3	#	$a [S.I$b s.n] $c 1977

PHYSICAL DESC.	#	#	$a 246p. $b $c $e
SERIES STATEMENT/ ADDED ENTRY-TITLE (440) (R)	#		$a $n
SERIES STATEMENT (490) (R)		#	$a
GENERAL NOTE (500) (R)	#	#	$a
CONTENTS NOTE (505) (R)		#	$a
SUBJECT ADDED ENTRY-PERSONAL NAME (600) (R)		0	$a $b $c
SUBJECT ADDED ENTRY-CORPORATE NAME (610) (R)		0	$a $c $d
SUBJECT ADDED ENTRY-TOPICAL NAME (650) (R)	#	0	$a English $v $x Spanish war $y $z
SUBJECT ADDED ENTRY-GEOGRAPHIC NAME (651) (R)		0	$a $v
ADDED ENTRY- PERSONAL NAME (700) (R)		#	$a $b $c
ADDED ENTRY- CORPORATE NAME (710) (R)		#	$a $b $c $d
ADDED ENTRY- MEETING NAME (711 (R)		#	$a $c $d

ADDED ENTRY – UNIFORM TITLE (730) (R)		#	$a
LOCATION (852)	1	#	$a
ACCESSION NO. INCL. DT. (901)			$a 48 $b 01-01-2005 $c
CALL NO. (902)			$a 940.2526 L77
SUBJECT HEADING DEFINED BY (903)			$a S.Das
ENTERED BY (904)			$a S.Das
VERIFIED BY (905)			$a S.Das

NB. #= Put blank. R means Repeatable. NR means Not Repeatable

EXAMPLE 47

ADVENTURES
of
Huckleberry Finn

Mark Twain

(pseudo)

Edited with an Introduction and Notes by

Emory Elliott

Oxford University Press

Oxford

1999

C.I - Description : iii, 284 page / ISBN:0 – 19 – 28241- 4 /
Series: Oxford World's Classics

MARC21: BIBLIOGRAPHIC FORMAT

LEADER (M):

n	a	m	a
Record Status	Type of record	Bibliographical level	Descriptive Catg.Form

CONTROL FIELD-MONOGRAPH & SERIAL (008)

t	1 9 9 9		o x n		g
Type of Date	Date1	Date2	Place of Publ.	Illustration	Target Audience

#						#	
Form Of Item	Nature of Contents	Govt. Pub.	Conf. Pub.	Festschrift	Index	Undefined	Literary Form

	e n g	#	
Biography	Language	Modified Record	Cata. Source

NAME OF THE FIELD INCL. MARC21 TAG	INDICATORS 1	2	DATA WITH SUBFIELD IDENTIFIERS
ISBN NO. (020) (R)	#	#	$a 0192824414 $c 155.00
ISSN (022) (R)	#	#	$a
DEWEY DECIMAL CLASSIFICATION NUMBER (082) (R)	0	#	$a 910.92 $b 20th ed
MAIN ENTRY-PERSONAL NAME (100) (NR)	1		$a Twain, M., pseudo. $b $c
MAIN ENTRY – CORPORATE NAME (110) NR		#	$a $b $c $d $n
MAIN ENTRY – MEETING name (111) (NR)		#	$a $c $d $e $n
MAIN ENTRY - UNIFORM TITLE (130) (NR)		#	$a $d $k $l $n
TITLA STATEMENT (245) (NR)			$a Adventures of huckleberry finn $b $c Mark Twain; edited with an introduction and note by Emory Eliot
EDITION STATEMENT (250) (nr)	#	#	$a $b
PUBLICATION DIST.	3	#	$a Oxford

ETC.(260) ®			$b Oxford University Press $c 1999
PHYSICAL DESC. (300) ®	#	#	$a iii, 284p. $b $c $e
SERIES STATEMENT/ ADDED ENTRY-TITLE (440) (R)	#		$a $n
SERIES STATEMENT (490) (R)		#	$a Oxford World's Classics
GENERAL NOTE (500) (R)	#	#	$a
CONTENTS NOTE (505) (R)		#	$a
SUBJECT ADDED ENTRY-PERSONAL NAME (600) (R)		0	$a $b $c
SUBJECT ADDED ENTRY-CORPORATE NAME (610) (R)	#	0	$a English Fiction $c $d
SUBJECT ADDED ENTRY-TOPICAL NAME (650) (R)		0	$a $v $x $y $z
SUBJECT ADDED ENTRY-GEOGRAPHIC NAME (651) (R)	#	0	$a $v
ADDED ENTRY- PERSONAL NAME (700) (R)	1	#	$a Eliot, Emory, ed. $b $c
ADDED ENTRY- CORPORATE NAME (710) (R)		#	$a $b $c $d

ADDED ENTRY- MEETING NAME (711 (R)		#	$a $c $d
ADDED ENTRY – UNIFORM TITLE (730) (R)		#	$a
LOCATION (852)	1	#	$a
ACCESSION NO. INCL. DT. (901)			$a 49 $b 01-01-2005 $c
CALL NO. (902)			$a 910.92 N99
SUBJECT HEADING DEFINED BY (903)			$a S.Das
ENTERED BY (904)			$a S.Das
VERIFIED BY (905)			$a S.Das

NB. #= Put blank. R means Repeatable. NR means Not Repeatable

EXAMPLE 47

Mark Twain : a lawral reader

Edited by

E. Fuller

1959

O.I. - Description:382 page / Subject - English

MARC21: BIBLIOGRAPHIC FORMAT

LEADER (M):

Record Status	Type of record	Bibliographical level	Descriptive Catg.Form
n	a	m	a

CONTROL FIELD-MONOGRAPH & SERIAL (008)

Type of Date	Date1	Date2	Place of Publ.	Illustration	Target Audience
t	1959		###		g

Form Of Item	Nature of Contents	Govt. Pub.	Conf. Pub.	Festschrift	Index	Undefined	Literary Form
#						#	

Biography	Language	Modified Record	Cata. Source
	eng	#	

NAME OF THE FIELD INCL. MARC21 TAG	INDICATORS 1	2	DATA WITH SUBFIELD IDENTIFIERS
ISBN NO. (020) (R)	#	#	$a 019852647 $c 160.00
ISSN (022) (R)	#	#	$a
DEWEY DECIMAL CLASSIFICATION NUMBER (082) (R)	0	#	$a 813 $b 20th ed
MAIN ENTRY-PERSONAL NAME (100) (NR)			$a $b $c
MAIN ENTRY – CORPORATE NAME (110) NR		#	$a $b $c $d $n
MAIN ENTRY – MEETING name (111) (NR)		#	$a $c $d $e $n
MAIN ENTRY - UNIFORM TITLE (130) (NR)		#	$a $d $k $l $n
TITLA STATEMENT (245) (NR)			$a Mark Twain $b a lawral reader $c edited by E. Fuller
EDITION STATEMENT (250) (nr)	#	#	$a $b
PUBLICATION DIST. ETC.(260) ®	3	#	$a [S.l $b s.n] $c 1959

PHYSICAL DESC. (300) ®	#	#	$a 382p. $b $c $e
SERIES STATEMENT/ ADDED ENTRY-TITLE (440) (R)	#		$a $n
SERIES STATEMENT (490) (R)		#	$a
GENERAL NOTE (500) (R)	#	#	$a
CONTENTS NOTE (505) (R)		#	$a
SUBJECT ADDED ENTRY-PERSONAL NAME (600) (R)		0	$a $b $c
SUBJECT ADDED ENTRY-CORPORATE NAME (610) (R)		0	$a $c $d
SUBJECT ADDED ENTRY-TOPICAL NAME (650) (R)	#	0	$a English $v $x $y $z
SUBJECT ADDED ENTRY-GEOGRAPHIC NAME (651) (R)	#	0	$a $v
ADDED ENTRY- PERSONAL NAME (700) (R)	1	#	$a Fuller, E., ed. $b $c
ADDED ENTRY- CORPORATE NAME (710) (R)		#	$a $b $c $d
ADDED ENTRY- MEETING NAME (711 (R)		#	$a $c $d

ADDED ENTRY – UNIFORM TITLE (730) (R)		#	$a
LOCATION (852)	1	#	$a
ACCESSION NO. INCL. DT. (901)			$a 50 $b 01-01-2005 $c
CALL NO. (902)			$a 813 J59
SUBJECT HEADING DEFINED BY (903)			$a S.Das
ENTERED BY (904)			$a S.Das
VERIFIED BY (905)			$a S.Das

NB. #= Put blank. R means Repeatable. NR means Not Repeatable

EXAMPLE 48

CANDIDE and Other Romances

Voltaire

(pseud)

Translate By :R. Aldington

with an

Introduction, Notes and Illustration by N. Tenlby

C 1956

O.I. - Description:144 page /

Subject - Comparative literature ; Romance

MARC21: BIBLIOGRAPHIC FORMAT

LEADER (M):

Record Status	Type of record	Bibliographical level	Descriptive Catg.Form
n	a	m	a

CONTROL FIELD-MONOGRAPH & SERIAL (008)

Type of Date	Date1	Date2	Place of Publ.	Illustration	Target Audience
t	1 9 5 6		# # #		g

Form Of Item	Nature of Contents	Govt. Pub.	Conf. Pub.	Festschrift	Index	Undefined	Literary Form
#						#	

Biography	Language	Modified Record	Cata. Source
	e n g	#	

NAME OF THE FIELD INCL. MARC21 TAG	INDICATORS 1	2	DATA WITH SUBFIELD IDENTIFIERS
ISBN NO. (020) (R)	#	#	$a 0119924562 $c 98.00
ISSN (022) (R)	#	#	$a
DEWEY DECIMAL CLASSIFICATION NUMBER (082) (R)	0	#	$a 808.8385 $b 20th ed
MAIN ENTRY-PERSONAL NAME (100) (NR)	#		$a Voltaire, pseud. $b $c
MAIN ENTRY – CORPORATE NAME (110) NR		#	$a $b $c $d $n
MAIN ENTRY – MEETING name (111) (NR)		#	$a $c $d $e $n
MAIN ENTRY - UNIFORM TITLE (130) (NR)		#	$a $d $k $l $n
TITLA STATEMENT (245) (NR)			$a Candide and other romances $b $c Voltaire; translated by R. Aldington
EDITION STATEMENT (250) (nr)	#	#	$a $b
PUBLICATION DIST. ETC.(260) ®	3	#	$a [S.l $b s.n]

			$c 1956
PHYSICAL DESC. (300) ®	#	#	$a 144p. $b $c $e
SERIES STATEMENT/ ADDED ENTRY-TITLE (440) (R)	#		$a $n
SERIES STATEMENT (490) (R)		#	$a
GENERAL NOTE (500) (R)	#	#	$a With an introduction, notes an illustration by N. Tenlby
CONTENTS NOTE (505) (R)		#	$a
SUBJECT ADDED ENTRY-PERSONAL NAME (600) (R)		0	$a $b $c
SUBJECT ADDED ENTRY-CORPORATE NAME (610) (R)		0	$a $c $d
SUBJECT ADDED ENTRY-TOPICAL NAME (650) (R)	#	0	$a Comparative literature $v $x Romance $y $z
SUBJECT ADDED ENTRY-GEOGRAPHIC NAME (651) (R)	#	0	$a $v
ADDED ENTRY-PERSONAL NAME (700) (R)	1	#	$a Aldington, R., ed. $b $c
ADDED ENTRY-CORPORATE NAME (710) (R)		#	$a $b $c $d

ADDED ENTRY- MEETING NAME (711) (R)		#	$a $c $d
ADDED ENTRY – UNIFORM TITLE (730) (R)		#	$a
LOCATION (852)	1	#	$a
ACCESSION NO. INCL. DT. (901)			$a 51 $b 01-01-2005 $c
CALL NO. (902)			$a 808.8385 J56
SUBJECT HEADING DEFINED BY (903)			$a S.Das
ENTERED BY (904)			$a S.Das
VERIFIED BY (905)			$a S.Das

NB. #= Put blank. R means Repeatable. NR means Not Repeatable

10

MARC 21: Bibliographic Format of Conference Proceedings

EXAMPLE 49

NEW ECONOMIC ORDER

Proceeding of International Economic Conference
held at Paris, April 3-12,1952

Edited By
Homer Tape Rosebergh

Academic Press

New York

1952

O.I. : 350 pages / Size - 26cm.

MARC21: BIBLIOGRAPHIC FORMAT

LEADER (M):

n	a	m	a
Record Status	Type of record	Bibliographical level	Descriptive Catg.Form

....

CONTROL FIELD-MONOGRAPH & SERIAL (008)

t	1 9 5 2		n y w		g
Type of Date	Date1	Date2	Place of Publ.	Illustration	Target Audience

#			1			#	
Form Of Item	Nature of Contents	Govt. Pub.	Conf. Pub.	Festschrift	Index	Undefined	Literary Form

	e n g	#	
Biography	Language	Modified Record	Cata. Source

....

NAME OF THE FIELD INCL. MARC21 TAG	INDICATORS 1	2	DATA WITH SUBFIELD IDENTIFIERS
ISBN NO. (020) (R)	#	#	$a $c 3.25 $
ISSN (022) (R)	#	#	$a
DEWEY DECIMAL CLASSIFICATION NUMBER (082) (R)	0	#	$a 330 $b 20th ed
MAIN ENTRY-PERSONAL NAME (100) (NR)			$a $b $c
MAIN ENTRY – CORPORATE NAME (110) NR		#	$a $b $c $d $n
MAIN ENTRY – MEETING name (111) (NR)	0	#	$a International Economic Conference $c Paris $d April 3-12, 1952 $e $n
MAIN ENTRY - UNIFORM TITLE (130) (NR)		#	$a $d $k $l $n
TITLA STATEMENT (245) (NR)			$a New economic order: $b proceedings of international economic conference $c edited by Homer Tape Rosenbergh
EDITION STATEMENT (250) (nr)	#	#	$a $b

PUBLICATION DIST. ETC.(260) ®	3	#	$a New York $b Academic Press $c 1952
PHYSICAL DESC. (300) ®	#	#	$a 350p. $b $c 26 cm. $e
SERIES STATEMENT/ ADDED ENTRY-TITLE (440) (R)	#		$a $n
SERIES STATEMENT (490) (R)		#	$a
GENERAL NOTE (500) (R)	#	#	$a
CONTENTS NOTE (505) (R)		#	$a
SUBJECT ADDED ENTRY-PERSONAL NAME (600) (R)		0	$a $b $c
SUBJECT ADDED ENTRY-CORPORATE NAME (610) (R)		0	$a $c $d
SUBJECT ADDED ENTRY-TOPICAL NAME (650) (R)	#	0	$a Economics $v $x $y $z
SUBJECT ADDED ENTRY-GEOGRAPHIC NAME (651) (R)	#	0	$a $v
ADDED ENTRY-PERSONAL NAME (700) (R)	1	#	$a Rosenbergh, Homer Tape, ed. $b $c
ADDED ENTRY-CORPORATE NAME (710) (R)		#	$a $b $c

		$d	
ADDED ENTRY- MEETING NAME (711 (R)		#	$a $c $d
ADDED ENTRY – UNIFORM TITLE (730) (R)		#	$a
LOCATION (852)	1	#	$a
ACCESSION NO. INCL. DT. (901)			$a 52 $b 01-01-2005 $c
CALL NO. (902)			$a 330 J52
SUBJECT HEADING DEFINED BY (903)			$a S.Das
ENTERED BY (904)			$a S.Das
VERIFIED BY (905)			$a S.Das

NB. #= Put blank. R means Repeatable. NR means Not Repeatable

EXAMPLE 50

Towards a new Marxism

(Proceedings of the First International Telos Conference)
(October 8-11, 1970)

Waterloo, Ontario

Edited By
Bart GrahlTelos Press,

USA

O.I.: 240p. / Size - 23cm

MARC21: BIBLIOGRAPHIC FORMAT

LEADER (M):

Record Status	Type of record	Bibliographical level	Descriptive Catg.Form
n	a	m	a

CONTROL FIELD-MONOGRAPH & SERIAL (008)

Type of Date	Date1	Date2	Place of Publ.	Illustration	Target Audience
t	1 9 7 0		u s #		g

Form Of Item	Nature of Contents	Govt. Pub.	Conf. Pub.	Festschrift	Index	Undefined	Literary Form
#			1			#	

Biography	Language	Modified Record	Cata. Source
	e n g	#	

NAME OF THE FIELD INCL. MARC21 TAG	INDICATORS 1	2	DATA WITH SUBFIELD IDENTIFIERS
ISBN NO. (020) (R)	#	#	$a $c 2.75$
ISSN (022) (R)	#	#	$a
DEWEY DECIMAL CLASSIFICATION NUMBER (082) (R)	0	#	$a 335.4 $b 20th ed
MAIN ENTRY-PERSONAL NAME (100) (NR)			$a $b $c
MAIN ENTRY –CORPORATE NAME (110) NR		#	$a $b $c $d $n
MAIN ENTRY – MEETING NAME (111) (NR)	0	#	$a International Telos Conference $c Waterloo, Ontario $d October 8-13, 1970 $e $n 1st
MAIN ENTRY - UNIFORM TITLE (130) (NR)		#	$a $d $k $l $n
TITLA STATEMENT (245) (NR)			$a Towards a new Marxism $b proceedings of first international Telos conference $c edited by Bart Grahl
EDITION STATEMENT (250) (nr)	#	#	$a $b

PUBLICATION DIST. ETC.(260) ®	3	#	$a USA $b Telos Press $c 1970
PHYSICAL DESC. (300) ®	#	#	$a 240p. $b $c 23 cm. $e
SERIES STATEMENT/ ADDED ENTRY-TITLE (440) (R)	#		$a $n
SERIES STATEMENT (490) (R)		#	$a
GENERAL NOTE (500) (R)	#	#	$a
CONTENTS NOTE (505) (R)		#	$a
SUBJECT ADDED ENTRY- PERSONAL NAME (600) (R)		0	$a $b $c
SUBJECT ADDED ENTRY- CORPORATE NAME (610) (R)		0	$a $c $d
SUBJECT ADDED ENTRY- TOPICAL NAME (650) (R)	#	0	$a Marxism Theory $v $x $y $z
SUBJECT ADDED ENTRY- GEOGRAPHIC NAME (651) (R)	#	0	$a $v
ADDED ENTRY- PERSONAL NAME (700) (R)		#	$a $b $c
ADDED ENTRY- CORPORATE NAME (710) (R)		#	$a $b $c $d

ADDED ENTRY- MEETING NAME (711 (R)		#	$a $c $d
ADDED ENTRY – UNIFORM TITLE (730) (R)		#	$a
LOCATION (852)	1	#	$a
ACCESSION NO. INCL. DT. (901)			$a 53 $b 01-01-2005 $c
CALL NO. (902)			$a 335.4 L70
SUBJECT HEADING DEFINED BY (903)			$a S.Das
ENTERED BY (904)			$a S.Das
VERIFIED BY (905)			$a S.Das

NB. #= Put blank. R means Repeatable. NR means Not Repeatable

EXAMPLE 51

A NATION IS BORN
(Papers presented at the International Seminar
on Bangladesh)
held in
Calcutta in April 1972

Executive Editor
Buddhadev Bhattacharya

Bangladesh Sahayak Samiti

Calcutta

1974

O.I.: 386p. / Size - 25cm

MARC21: BIBLIOGRAPHIC FORMAT

LEADER (M):

Record Status	Type of record	Bibliographical level	Descriptive Catg.Form
n	a	m	a

CONTROL FIELD-MONOGRAPH & SERIAL (008)

Type of Date	Date1	Date2	Place of Publ.	Illustration	Target Audience
t	1 9 7 4		k o i		g

Form Of Item	Nature of Contents	Govt. Pub.	Conf. Pub.	Festschrift	Index	Undefined	Literary Form
#			1			#	

Biography	Language	Modified Record	Cata. Source
	e n g	#	

NAME OF THE FIELD INCL. MARC21 TAG	INDICATORS 1	2	DATA WITH SUBFIELD IDENTIFIERS
ISBN NO. (020) (R)	#	#	$a $c Rs. 50.00
ISSN (022) (R)	#	#	$a
DEWEY DECIMAL CLASSIFICATION NUMBER (082) (R)	0	#	$a 954.92 $b 20th ed
MAIN ENTRY-PERSONAL NAME (100) (NR)			$a $b $c
MAIN ENTRY –CORPORATE NAME (110) NR		#	$a $b $c $d $n
MAIN ENTRY – MEETING name (111) (NR)	0	#	$a International Seminar on Bangladesh $c Kolkata $d April, 1972 $e $n
MAIN ENTRY - UNIFORM TITLE (130) (NR)		#	$a $d $k $l $n
TITLA STATEMENT (245) (NR)			$a A nation is born $b papers presented on the international seminar on Bangladesh $c edited by Buddhadeb Bhattacharyya
EDITION STATEMENT (250) (nr)	#	#	$a $b

PUBLICATION DIST. ETC.(260) ®	3	#	$a Kolkata $b Bangladesh Sahayak Parisad $c 1974
PHYSICAL DESC. (300) ®	#	#	$a 386p. $b $c 25 cm. $e
SERIES STATEMENT/ ADDED ENTRY-TITLE (440) (R)	#		$a $n
SERIES STATEMENT (490) (R)		#	$a
GENERAL NOTE (500) (R)	#	#	$a
CONTENTS NOTE (505) (R)		#	$a
SUBJECT ADDED ENTRY-PERSONAL NAME (600) (R)		0	$a $b $c
SUBJECT ADDED ENTRY-CORPORATE NAME (610) (R)		0	$a $c $d
SUBJECT ADDED ENTRY-TOPICAL NAME (650) (R)		0	$a $v $x $y $z
SUBJECT ADDED ENTRY-GEOGRAPHIC NAME (651) (R)	#	0	$a Bangladesh $v History
ADDED ENTRY- PERSONAL NAME (700) (R)	1	#	$a Bhattacharyya, Buddhadeb, ed. $b $c
ADDED ENTRY- CORPORATE NAME (710) (R)		#	$a $b

			$c $d
ADDED ENTRY- MEETING NAME (711 (R)		#	$a $c $d
ADDED ENTRY – UNIFORM TITLE (730) (R)		#	$a
LOCATION (852)	1	#	$a
ACCESSION NO. INCL. DT. (901)			$a 54 $b 01-01-2005 $c
CALL NO. (902)			$a 954.92 L74
SUBJECT HEADING DEFINED BY (903)			$a S.Das
ENTERED BY (904)			$a S.Das
VERIFIED BY (905)			$a S.Das

NB. #= Put blank. R means Repeatable. NR means Not Repeatable

EXAMPLE 52

Netaji and India's Freedom: Proceeding of the International Netaji Seminar, 1973

Edited By

Sisir Kumar Bose

Calcutta

Netaji Bhaban

1975

O.I. - 472p./ Height - 25cm

MARC21: BIBLIOGRAPHIC FORMAT

LEADER (M):

Record Status	Type of record	Bibliographical level	Descriptive Catg.Form
n	a	m	a

CONTROL FIELD-MONOGRAPH & SERIAL (008)

Type of Date	Date1	Date2	Place of Publ.	Illustration	Target Audience
t	1 9 7 3		k o i		g

Form Of Item	Nature of Contents	Govt. Pub.	Conf. Pub.	Festschrift	Index	Undefined	Literary Form
#			1			#	

Biography	Language	Modified Record	Cata. Source
	e n g	#	

NAME OF THE FIELD INCL. MARC21 TAG	INDICATORS 1	2	DATA WITH SUBFIELD IDENTIFIERS
ISBN NO. (020) (R)	#	#	$a $c Rs. 60.00
ISSN (022) (R)	#	#	$a
DEWEY DECIMAL CLASSIFICATION NUMBER (082) (R)	0	#	$a 954.035 $b 20th ed
MAIN ENTRY-PERSONAL NAME (100) (NR)			$a $b $c
MAIN ENTRY –CORPORATE NAME (110) NR		#	$a $b $c $d $n
MAIN ENTRY – MEETING name (111) (NR)	0	#	$a International Netaji seminar $c Kolkata $d 1973 $e $n
MAIN ENTRY - UNIFORM TITLE (130) (NR)		#	$a $d $k $l $n
TITLA STATEMENT (245) (NR)			$a Netaji an India's freedom $b proceedings of the international Netaji seminar $c edited by Sisir Kumar Bose
EDITION STATEMENT (250) (nr)	#	#	$a $b

PUBLICATION DIST. ETC.(260) ®	3	#	$a Kolkata $b Netaji Bhaban $c 1973
PHYSICAL DESC. (300) ®	#	#	$a 427p. $b $c 25 cm. $e
SERIES STATEMENT/ ADDED ENTRY-TITLE (440) (R)	#		$a $n
SERIES STATEMENT (490) (R)		#	$a
GENERAL NOTE (500) (R)	#	#	$a
CONTENTS NOTE (505) (R)		#	$a
SUBJECT ADDED ENTRY-PERSONAL NAME (600) (R)	1	0	$a Bose, Subhas Chandra $b $c Netaji
SUBJECT ADDED ENTRY-CORPORATE NAME (610) (R)		0	$a $c $d
SUBJECT ADDED ENTRY-TOPICAL NAME (650) (R)		0	$a $v $x $y $z
SUBJECT ADDED ENTRY-GEOGRAPHIC NAME (651) (R)	#	0	$a India $v History
ADDED ENTRY-PERSONAL NAME (700) (R)	1	#	$a Bose, Sisir Kumar, ed. $b $c
ADDED ENTRY-CORPORATE NAME (710) (R)		#	$a $b $c

			$d
ADDED ENTRY- MEETING NAME (711 (R)		#	$a $c $d
ADDED ENTRY – UNIFORM TITLE (730) (R)		#	$a
LOCATION (852)	1	#	$a
ACCESSION NO. INCL. DT. (901)			$a 55 $b 01-01-2005 $c
CALL NO. (902)			$a 950.035 L73
SUBJECT HEADING DEFINED BY (903)			$a S.Das
ENTERED BY (904)			$a S.Das
VERIFIED BY (905)			$a S.Das

NB. #= Put blank. R means Repeatable. NR means Not Repeatable

EXAMPLE 53

Proceeding of the Conference on Knowledge Management
(held at Mysore, August 2-5, 1989)

Edited By

Dr. Shalini Urs

(School of Information Management)

University of Mysore

Mysore

1990

O.I.: Pages 237/ Height - 24cm.

MARC21: BIBLIOGRAPHIC FORMAT

LEADER (M):

Record Status	Type of record	Bibliographical level	Descriptive Catg.Form
n	a	m	a

CONTROL FIELD-MONOGRAPH & SERIAL (008)

Type of Date	Date1	Date2	Place of Publ.	Illustration	Target Audience
t	1 9 9 0		m y i		g

Form Of Item	Nature of Contents	Govt. Pub.	Conf. Pub.	Festschrift	Index	Undefined	Literary Form
#			1			#	

Biography	Language	Modified Record	Cata. Source
	e n g	#	

NAME OF THE FIELD INCL. MARC21 TAG	INDICATORS 1	2	DATA WITH SUBFIELD IDENTIFIERS
ISBN NO. (020) (R)	#	#	$a $c
ISSN (022) (R)	#	#	$a
DEWEY DECIMAL CLASSIFICATION NUMBER (082) (R)	0	#	$a 025.4 $b 20th ed
MAIN ENTRY-PERSONAL NAME (100) (NR)			$a $b $c
MAIN ENTRY –CORPORATE NAME (110) NR		#	$a $b $c $d $n
MAIN ENTRY – MEETING name (111) (NR)	0	#	$a Conference on knowledge management $c Mysore $d August, 2-5, 1989 $e $n
MAIN ENTRY - UNIFORM TITLE (130) (NR)		#	$a $d $k $l $n
TITLA STATEMENT (245) (NR)			$a Proceeding on conference on knowledge management $b $c edited by Shalini Urs
EDITION STATEMENT (250) (nr)	#	#	$a $b

PUBLICATION DIST. ETC.(260) ®	3	#	$a Mysore $b University of Mysore, School of Information Management $c 1990
PHYSICAL DESC. (300) ®	#	#	$a 237p. $b $c 24 cm. $e
SERIES STATEMENT/ ADDED ENTRY-TITLE (440) (R)	#		$a $n
SERIES STATEMENT (490) (R)		#	$a
GENERAL NOTE (500) (R)	#	#	$a
CONTENTS NOTE (505) (R)		#	$a
SUBJECT ADDED ENTRY-PERSONAL NAME (600) (R)		0	$a $b $c
SUBJECT ADDED ENTRY-CORPORATE NAME (610) (R)	2	0	$a University of Mysore, School of Information Management $c $d
SUBJECT ADDED ENTRY-TOPICAL NAME (650) (R)		0	$a Classification $v $x $y $z
SUBJECT ADDED ENTRY-GEOGRAPHIC NAME (651) (R)	#	0	$a $v
ADDED ENTRY- PERSONAL NAME (700) (R)	1	#	$a Urs, Shalini, ed. $b $c
ADDED ENTRY-		#	$a

CORPORATE NAME (710) (R)			$b $c $d
ADDED ENTRY-MEETING NAME (711 (R)		#	$a $c $d
ADDED ENTRY – UNIFORM TITLE (730) (R)		#	$a
LOCATION (852)	1	#	$a
ACCESSION NO. INCL. DT. (901)			$a 56 $b 01-01-2005 $c
CALL NO. (902)			$a 025.4 M89
SUBJECT HEADING DEFINED BY (903)			$a S.Das
ENTERED BY (904)			$a S.Das
VERIFIED BY (905)			$a S.Das

NB. #= Put blank. R means Repeatable. NR means Not Repeatable

11

MARC 21: Bibliographic Format of Non-book Materials

EXAMPLE 54

COAL

Plant life to plastics

Washington, D.C.

Bituminous Coal Institute, Education Department

1967

O.I.: 1 exhibit in 12 pieces. Coloured in folds 25×17×2 cm.
This realia contains sample of coal & coal products.

MARC21: BIBLIOGRAPHIC FORMAT

LEADER (M):

n	r	m	a
Record Status	Type of record	Bibliographical level	Descriptive Catg.Form

....

CONTROL FIELD –MONOGRAPH & SERIAL (008)

t	1 9 6 7		w a n	a	f
Type of Date	Date1	Date2	Place of Publ.	Illustration	Target Audience

#							#	
Form Of Item	Nature of Contents	Govt. Pub.	Conf. Pub.	Festschrift	Index	Undefined	Literary Form

	e n g	#	
Biography	Language	Modified Record	Cata. Source

....

NAME OF THE FIELD INCL. MARC21 TAG	INDICATORS 1	2	DATA WITH SUBFIELD IDENTIFIERS
ISBN NO. (020) (R)	#	#	$a $c
ISSN (022) (R)			$a
DEWEY DECIMAL CLASSIFICATION NUMBER (082) (R)	0	#	$a 622.3 34 $b 20th ed
MAIN ENTRY-PERSONAL NAME (100) (NR)			$a $b $c
MAIN ENTRY – CORPORATE NAME (110) NR			$a $b $c $d $n
MAIN ENTRY – MEETING name (111) (NR)			$a $c $d $e $n
MAIN ENTRY - UNIFORM TITLE (130) (NR)			$a $d $k $l $n
KEY TITLE(222)			$a $b
TITLE STATEMENT (245) (NR)			$a Coal [realia] : plants life to plastics $c
EDITION STATEMENT (250) (nr)	#	#	$a
PUBLICATION DIST.	3	#	$a Washington, D.C.

ETC.(260) ®			$b Bituminous Coal Institute, Education Dept. $c 1967
PHYSICAL DESC. (300) ®	#	#	$a 1 exhibit (12 pieces) $b col. $c 25×17×2 cm$e
SERIES STATEMENT/ ADDED ENTRY-TITLE (440) (R)	#		$a
SERIES STATEMENT (490)(R)			$a
GENERAL NOTE (500) (R)	#	#	$a Sample of coal and coal product
CONTENTS NOTE (505)(R)			$a
SUBJECT ADDED ENTRY-PERSONAL NAME (600) (R)			$a $b $c
SUBJECT ADDED ENTRY-CORPORATE NAME (610) (R)			$a $c $d
SUBJECT ADDED ENTRY-TOPICAL NAME (650) (R)	#	0	$a Virtual reality $v $x $y $z
SUBJECT ADDED ENTRY-GEOGRAPHIC NAME (651) (R)			$a $v
ADDED ENTRY- PERSONAL NAME (700) (R)			$a $b $c
ADDED ENTRY-CORPORATE NAME (710) (R)			$a Education Department $b Bituminous Coal Institute

			\$c \$d
ADDED ENTRY- MEETING NAME (711 (R)			\$a \$c \$d
ADDED ENTRY – UNIFORM TITLE (730) (R)			\$a
LOCATION (852)	1	#	\$a
ACCESSION NO. INCL. DT. (901)			\$a 57 \$b 6-10-07 \$c
CALL NO. (902)			\$a 622.334 K67
SUBJECT HEADING DEFINED BY (903)			\$a S.Das
ENTERED BY (904)			\$a S.Das
VERIFIED BY (905)			\$a S.Das

NB. #= Put blank. R means Repeatable. NR means Not Repeatable

EXAMPLE 55

ROCKY MOUNTAIN HIGH

John Denver

New York

RCA Victor

1972

O.I.: Side 1, Stereo, LSP-4731. Duration of sound disc 32 minutes and analog having 33 1/3 rpm. Songs/ John Denver accompanying himself on the 6 or 12 string guitar, Instrumental and Vocal ensemble. Text on album. Content of the text – Rocky Mountain High/John Denver with Mike Taylor (4:41).

MARC21: BIBLIOGRAPHIC FORMAT

LEADER (M):

n	j	m	a
Record Status	**Type of record**	**Bibliographical level**	**Descriptive Catg.Form**

CONTROL FIELD –MONOGRAPH & SERIAL (008)

t	1 9 7 2		n y u	a	f
Type of Date	**Date1**	**Date2**	**Place of Publ.**	**Illustration**	**Target Audience**

#							#	
Form Of Item	**Nature of Contents**	**Govt. Pub.**	**Conf. Pub.**	**Festschrift**	**Index**	**Undefined**	**Literary Form**

	e n g	#	
Biography	**Language**	**Modified Record**	**Cata. Source**

NAME OF THE FIELD INCL. MARC21 TAG	INDICATORS 1	2	DATA WITH SUBFIELD IDENTIFIERS
ISBN NO. (020) (R)	#	#	$a $c
ISSN (022) (R)			$a
DEWEY DECIMAL CLASSIFICATION NUMBER (082) (R)	0	#	$a 900 $b 20th ed
MAIN ENTRY-PERSONAL NAME (100) (NR)			$a Denver, John $b $c
MAIN ENTRY –CORPORATE NAME (110) NR			$a $b $c $d $n
MAIN ENTRY – MEETING name (111) (NR)			$a $c $d $e $n
MAIN ENTRY - UNIFORM TITLE (130) (NR)			$a $d $k $l $n
KEY TITLE(222)			$a $b
TITLE STATEMENT (245) (NR)			$a Rocky mountain high[sound recording] $c
EDITION STATEMENT (250) (nr)		#	# $a
PUBLICATION DIST. ETC.(260) ®	3	#	$a New York $b RCA Victor

			$c 1972
PHYSICAL DESC. (300) ®	#	#	$a On 1 side of 1 sound disc (32 min.) $b analog $c 33 $^{1/3}$ rpm $e stereo
SERIES STATEMENT/ ADDED ENTRY-TITLE (440) (R)	#		$a
SERIES STATEMENT (490)(R)			$a
GENERAL NOTE (500) (R)	#	#	$a Songs: John Denver accompanying himself on the 6 or 12 string guitar, instrumental and vocal ensemble. – Text on album
CONTENTS NOTE (505)(R)			$a Rocky mountain high/ John Denver with Mike Taylor (4:41). – RCA Victor: LSP 4731
SUBJECT ADDED ENTRY- PERSONAL NAME (600) (R)			$a $b $c
SUBJECT ADDED ENTRY-CORPORATE NAME (610) (R)			$a $c $d
SUBJECT ADDED ENTRY-TOPICAL NAME (650) (R)	#	0	$a Sound discs $v $x $y $z
SUBJECT ADDED ENTRY-GEOGRAPHIC NAME (651) (R)			$a Rocky Mountain $v
ADDED ENTRY- PERSONAL			$a

NAME (700) (R)			$b $c
ADDED ENTRY- CORPORATE NAME (710) (R)			$a $b $c $d
ADDED ENTRY- MEETING NAME (711 (R)			$a $c $d
ADDED ENTRY – UNIFORM TITLE (730) (R)			$a
LOCATION (852)	1	#	$a
ACCESSION NO. INCL. DT. (901)			$a 58 $b 6-10-07 $c
CALL NO. (902)			$a 900 L72
SUBJECT HEADING DEFINED BY (903)			$a S.Das
ENTERED BY (904)			$a S.Das
VERIFIED BY (905)			$a S.Das

NB. #= Put blank. R means Repeatable. NR means Not Repeatable

EXAMPLE 56

THE DEATH OF THE NARGIN

Phillip Gallie
1957

O.I.: The Death of the Nargin 1 art print. B and w engraving 31´42 cm. This graphic material is based on the Tempera Painting by Pieter Brueghel the elder.

MARC21: BIBLIOGRAPHIC FORMAT

LEADER (M):

n	p	m	a
Record Status	**Type of record**	**Bibliographical level**	**Descriptive Catg.Form**

CONTROL FIELD –MONOGRAPH & SERIAL (008)

n			a	f
Type of Date	**Date1**	**Date2**	**Place of Publ.**	**Illustration**	**Target Audience**

#						#	
Form Of Item	**Nature of Contents**	**Govt. Pub.**	**Conf. Pub.**	**Festschrift**	**Index**	**Undefined**	**Literary Form**

	e n g	#	
Biography	**Language**	**Modified Record**	**Cata. Source**

NAME OF THE FIELD INCL. MARC21 TAG	INDICATORS 1	2	DATA WITH SUBFIELD IDENTIFIERS
ISBN NO. (020) ®	#	#	$a $c
ISSN (022) ®			$a
DEWEY DECIMAL CLASSIFICATION NUMBER (082) ®	0	#	$a 808.80359 $b 20th ed
MAIN ENTRY-PERSONAL NAME (100) (NR)			$a Gallie, Phillip $b $c
MAIN ENTRY –CORPORATE NAME (110) (NR)			$a $b $c $d $n
MAIN ENTRY – MEETING name (111) (NR)			$a $c $d $e $n
MAIN ENTRY – UNIFORM TITLE (130) (NR)			$a $d $k $l $n
KEY TITLE(222)			$a $b
TITLE STATEMENT (245) (NR)			$a The death of the nargin [Graphic materials] $c
EDITION STATEMENT (250) (nr)	#	#	$a

PUBLICATION DIST. ETC.(260) ®	3	#	$a [S.l. $b s.n.] $c
PHYSICAL DESC. (300) ®	#	#	$a 1 art print $b b and w engraving $c 31×42 cm $e
SERIES STATEMENT/ ADDED ENTRY-TITLE (440) ®	#		$a
SERIES STATEMENT (490)®			$a
GENERAL NOTE (500) ®	#	#	$a Based on the Tempera painting by Pieter Brueghel the elder
CONTENTS NOTE (505)®			$a
SUBJECT ADDED ENTRY-PERSONAL NAME (600) ®			$a $b $c
SUBJECT ADDED ENTRY-CORPORATE NAME (610) ®			$a $c $d
SUBJECT ADDED ENTRY-TOPICAL NAME (650) ®	#	0	$a Graphics arts $v $x $y $z
SUBJECT ADDED ENTRY-GEOGRAPHIC NAME (651) ®			$a $v
ADDED ENTRY-PERSONAL NAME (700) ®			$a $b $c
ADDED ENTRY- CORPORATE			$a

NAME (710) ®			$b $c $d
ADDED ENTRY- MEETING NAME (711 ®			$a $c $d
ADDED ENTRY – UNIFORM TITLE (730) ®			$a
LOCATION (852)	1	#	$a
ACCESSION NO. INCL. DT. (901)			$a 59 $b 6-10-07 $c
CALL NO. (902)			$a 808.80354 J57
SUBJECT HEADING DEFINED BY (903)			$a S.Das
ENTERED BY (904)			$a S.Das
VERIFIED BY (905)			$a S.Das

NB. #= Put blank. R means Repeatable. NR means Not Repeatable

EXAMPLE 57

RENAISSANCE CORAL MUSIC FOR HAPPY X-MAS

Jacob Gallus

New York

Macmillan

1965

O.I.: Duration of sound disc 35 minutes of analog, rpm 33 1/3 stereo. A camerate recording. Macmillan records – H-70891. Songs in German language or Latin language. N.C.R.V. Vocal ensemble Marinus Voorberg. Text with English translations, on container. Contents – Praeter retum seriem by Josquin Desperz (6:51).

MARC21: BIBLIOGRAPHIC FORMAT

LEADER (M):

n	j	m	a
Record Status	Type of record	Bibliographical level	Descriptive Catg.Form

CONTROL FIELD –MONOGRAPH & SERIAL (008)

t	1 9 6 5		n y u	#	f
Type of Date	Date1	Date2	Place of Publ.	Illustration	Target Audience

#							#	
Form Of Item	Nature of Contents	Govt. Pub.	Conf. Pub.	Festschrift	Index	Undefined	Literary Form

	e n g	#	
Biography	Language	Modified Record	Cata. Source

NAME OF THE FIELD INCL. MARC21 TAG	INDICATORS 1	2	DATA WITH SUBFIELD IDENTIFIERS
ISBN NO. (020) (R)	#	#	$a $c
ISSN (022) (R)			$a
DEWEY DECIMAL CLASSIFICATION NUMBER (082) (R)	0	#	$a 781.7102 $b 20th ed
MAIN ENTRY-PERSONAL NAME (100) (NR)			$a Gallus, Jacob $b $c
MAIN ENTRY –CORPORATE NAME (110) NR			$a $b $c $d $n
MAIN ENTRY – MEETING name (111) (NR)			$a $c $d $e $n
MAIN ENTRY - UNIFORM TITLE (130) (NR)			$a $d $k $l $n
KEY TITLE(222)			$a $b
TITLE STATEMENT (245) (NR)			$a Renaissance coral music for happy x-mas [sound recording] $c
EDITION STATEMENT (250) (nr)	#	#	$a

PUBLICATION DIST. ETC.(260) ®	3	#	$a New York $b Macmillan $c 1965
PHYSICAL DESC. (300) ®	#	#	$a 1 sound disc (35 min.) $b analog $c 33 1/3 rpm $e stereo
SERIES STATEMENT/ ADDED ENTRY-TITLE (440) (R)	#		$a
SERIES STATEMENT (490)(R)			$a
GENERAL NOTE (500) (R)	#	#	$a Came rate recording. – Songs in German or Latin. – N.C.R.V. vocal ensemble Marinus Voorberg. – Text with English translations on container
CONTENTS NOTE (505)(R)			$a Practer retum seriem by Josquin Desprez (6: 51) . – Macmillan Record : H 70891
SUBJECT ADDED ENTRY-PERSONAL NAME (600) (R)			$a $b $c
SUBJECT ADDED ENTRY-CORPORATE NAME (610) (R)			$a $c $d
SUBJECT ADDED ENTRY-TOPICAL NAME (650) (R)	#	0	$a Sound discs $v $x $y $z
SUBJECT ADDED ENTRY-GEOGRAPHIC NAME (651) (R)			$a $v

ADDED ENTRY- PERSONAL NAME (700) (R)			$a $b $c
ADDED ENTRY- CORPORATE NAME (710) (R)			$a $b $c $d
ADDED ENTRY- MEETING NAME (711 (R)			$a $c $d
ADDED ENTRY – UNIFORM TITLE (730) (R)			$a
LOCATION (852)	1	#	$a
ACCESSION NO. INCL. DT. (901)			$a 60 $b 6-10-07 $c
CALL NO. (902)			$a 781.7102 K65
SUBJECT HEADING DEFINED BY (903)			$a S.Das
ENTERED BY (904)			$a S.Das
VERIFIED BY (905)			$a S.Das

NB. #= Put blank. R means Repeatable. NR means Not Repeatable

EXAMPLE 58

GENESIS OF NOVEL

A Documentary on the writing regimen of George Simenon

Tucson

Motivational Programming Corporation

1969

O.I.: Sound cassette analog having duration 24 minutes. 2 track and mono under 20th century European authors.

MARC21: BIBLIOGRAPHIC FORMAT

LEADER (M):

Record Status	Type of record	Bibliographical level	Descriptive Catg.Form
n	j	m	a

CONTROL FIELD –MONOGRAPH & SERIAL (008)

Type of Date	Date1	Date2	Place of Publ.	Illustration	Target Audience
t	1 9 6 9		t u #	#	f

Form Of Item	Nature of Contents	Govt. Pub.	Conf. Pub.	Festschrift	Index	Undefined	Literary Form
#						#	

Biography	Language	Modified Record	Cata. Source
	e n g	#	

NAME OF THE FIELD INCL. MARC21 TAG	INDICATORS 1	2	DATA WITH SUBFIELD IDENTIFIERS
ISBN NO. (020) (R)	#	#	$a $c
ISSN (022) (R)	#		$a
DEWEY DECIMAL CLASSIFICATION NUMBER (082) (R)	0	#	$a 808.3 $b 20th ed
MAIN ENTRY-PERSONAL NAME (100) (NR)			$a $b $c
MAIN ENTRY –CORPORATE NAME (110) NR			$a $b $c $d $n
MAIN ENTRY – MEETING name (111) (NR)			$a $c $d $e $n
MAIN ENTRY - UNIFORM TITLE (130) (NR)			$a $d $k $l $n
KEY TITLE(222)			$a $b
TITLE STATEMENT (245) (NR)			$a Genesis of novel [sound recording]: a documentary on the writing regimen of George Simenon $c

EDITION STATEMENT (250) (nr)	#	#	$a
PUBLICATION DIST. ETC.(260) ®	3	#	$a Tucson $b Motivational Programming Corporation $c 1969
PHYSICAL DESC. (300) ®	#	#	$a 1 sound cassette (24 min.) $b analog $c 2 track $e mono.
SERIES STATEMENT/ ADDED ENTRY-TITLE (440) (R)	#		$a 20th century European author
SERIES STATEMENT (490)(R)			$a 20th century European author
GENERAL NOTE (500) (R)	#	#	$a
CONTENTS NOTE (505)(R)			$a
SUBJECT ADDED ENTRY-PERSONAL NAME (600) (R)			$a $b $c
SUBJECT ADDED ENTRY-CORPORATE NAME (610) (R)			$a $c $d
SUBJECT ADDED ENTRY-TOPICAL NAME (650) (R)	#	0	$a Sound discs $v $x $y $z
SUBJECT ADDED ENTRY-GEOGRAPHIC NAME (651) (R)			$a $v
ADDED ENTRY- PERSONAL NAME (700) (R)			$a $b $c

ADDED ENTRY- CORPORATE NAME (710) (R)			$a Motivational Programming Corporation, Tucson $b $c $d
ADDED ENTRY- MEETING NAME (711 (R)			$a $c $d
ADDED ENTRY – UNIFORM TITLE (730) (R)			$a
LOCATION (852)	1	#	$a
ACCESSION NO. INCL. DT. (901)			$a 61 $b 6-10-07 $c
CALL NO. (902)			$a 808.3 K69
SUBJECT HEADIN EFINE D BY (903)			$a S.Das
ENTERED BY (904)			$a S.Das
VERIFIED BY (905)			$a S.Das

NB. #= Put blank. R means Repeatable. NR means Not Repeatable

EXAMPLE 59

WORLD
Political cum Commercial
(with air and sea routes)
MAP

Government of India

Chandigarh

Bharat Graphics

1995

O.I.: Scale ca.1:33 million approx. Size: 95´64 cm. Copyright: Government of India

MARC21: BIBLIOGRAPHIC FORMAT

LEADER (M):

n	e	m	a
Record Status	Type of record	Bibliographical level	Descriptive Catg.Form

CONTROL FIELD –MONOGRAPH & SERIAL (008)

t	1 9 9 5		c h i	a	f
Type of Date	Date1	Date2	Place of Publ.	Illustration	Target Audience

#						#	
Form Of Item	Nature of Contents	Govt. Pub.	Conf. Pub.	Festschrift	Index	Undefined	Literary Form

	e n g	#	
Biography	Language	Modified Record	Cata. Source

NAME OF THE FIELD INCL. MARC21 TAG	INDICATORS 1	2	DATA WITH SUBFIELD IDENTIFIERS
ISBN NO. (020) ®	#	#	$a $c
ISSN (022) ®			$a
DEWEY DECIMAL CLASSIFICATION NUMBER (082) ®	0	#	$a 912 $b 20th ed
MAIN ENTRY-PERSONAL NAME (100) (NR)			$a $b $c
MAIN ENTRY –CORPORATE NAME (110) NR			$a India $b Government of India $c $d $n
MAIN ENTRY – MEETING name (111) (NR)			$a $c $d $e $n
MAIN ENTRY – UNIFORM TITLE (130) (NR)			$a $d $k $l $n
KEY TITLE(222)			$a $b
TITLE STATEMENT (245) (NR)			$a World [map] : political cum commercial (with air and sea route) $c
EDITION STATEMENT (250) (nr)	#	#	$a

PUBLICATION DIST. ETC.(260) ®	3	#	$a Chandigarh $b Bharat Graphics $c 1995
PHYSICAL DESC. (300) ®	#	#	$a 1 map $b : col. $c 95×64 cm $e
SCALE			Ca.1:33million approx.
SERIES STATEMENT/ ADDED ENTRY-TITLE (440) ®	#		$a
SERIES STATEMENT (490)®			$a
GENERAL NOTE (500) ®	#	#	$a
CONTENTS NOTE (505)®			$a
SUBJECT ADDED ENTRY-PERSONAL NAME (600) ®			$a $b $c
SUBJECT ADDED ENTRY-CORPORATE NAME (610) ®			$a $c $d
SUBJECT ADDED ENTRY-TOPICAL NAME (650) ®	#	0	$a World-map $v $x $y $z
SUBJECT ADDED ENTRY-GEOGRAPHIC NAME (651) ®			$a $v
ADDED ENTRY- PERSONAL NAME (700) ®			$a $b $c
ADDED ENTRY- CORPORATE NAME (710) ®			$a $b $c $d

ADDED ENTRY- MEETING NAME (711 ®			$a $c $d
ADDED ENTRY – UNIFORM TITLE (730) ®			$a
LOCATION (852)	1	#	$a
ACCESSION NO. INCL. DT. (901)			$a 62 $b 7-10-07 $c
CALL NO. (902)			$a 912 N95
SUBJECT HEADING EFINED BY (903)			$a S.Das
ENTERED BY (904)			$a S.Das
VERIFIED BY (905)			$a S.Das

NB. #= Put blank. R means Repeatable. NR means Not Repeatable

EXAMPLE 60

AN INTRODUCTION TO OPERATING SYSTEM
Computer Program

London

Zenith Software Inc.

1994

O.I.: 1 computer disk $5^{1/4}$ in manual, having illustrations. Height – 22 cm. 5 pages. The Zenith Series. The DOS tutorial program. System requirements – IBM PC, XT, PC Jr DOS 2.1 or greater 80 columns monitor. 1 double sided disk drive. The title from the disk label. Includes function key template.

MARC21: BIBLIOGRAPHIC FORMAT

LEADER (M):

Record Status	Type of record	Bibliographical level	Descriptive Catg.Form
n	m	m	a

CONTROL FIELD –MONOGRAPH & SERIAL (008)

Type of Date	Date1	Date2	Place of Publ.	Illustration	Target Audience
t	1 9 9 4		l o #	a	f

Form Of Item	Nature of Contents	Govt. Pub.	Conf. Pub.	Festschrift	Index	Undefined	Literary Form
#						#	

Biography	Language	Modified Record	Cata. Source
	e n g	#	

NAME OF THE FIELD INCL. MARC21 TAG	INDICATORS 1	2	DATA WITH SUBFIELD IDENTIFIERS
ISBN NO. (020) (R)	#	#	$a $c
ISSN (022) (R)			$a
DEWEY DECIMAL CLASSIFICATION NUMBER (082) (R)	0	#	$a 005.43 $b 20th ed
MAIN ENTRY-PERSONAL NAME (100) (NR)			$a $b $c
MAIN ENTRY –CORPORATE NAME (110) NR			$a $b $c $d $n
MAIN ENTRY – MEETING name (111) (NR)			$a $c $d $e $n
MAIN ENTRY - UNIFORM TITLE (130) (NR)			$a $d $k $l $n
KEY TITLE(222)			$a $b
TITLE STATEMENT (245) (NR)			$a An introduction to operating system [computer file] $c
EDITION STATEMENT (250) (nr)	#	#	$a

PUBLICATION DIST. ETC.(260) ®	3	#	$a London $b Zenith Software $c 1994
PHYSICAL DESC. (300) ®	#	#	$a 1 computer disc; 5 ¼ in.+1 manual (5p.) $b ill. $c 22cm. $e
SERIES STATEMENT/ ADDED ENTRY-TITLE (440) (R)	#		$a The Zenith Series
SERIES STATEMENT (490)(R)			$a The Zenith Series
GENERAL NOTE (500) (R)	#	#	$a The DOS tutorial program. – System requirements: IBM PC*T PC Jr DOS 2.1 or grater 80 column monitor; 1 double sided disc drive. – Title from the disc label. – Includes function key template
CONTENTS NOTE (505)(R)			$a
SUBJECT ADDED ENTRY-PERSONAL NAME (600) (R)			$a $b $c
SUBJECT ADDED ENTRY-CORPORATE NAME (610) (R)			$a $c $d
SUBJECT ADDED ENTRY-TOPICAL NAME (650) (R)	#	0	$a Computer operating system $v $x $y $z
SUBJECT ADDED ENTRY-GEOGRAPHIC NAME			$a $v

(651) (R)			
ADDED ENTRY- PERSONAL NAME (700) (R)			$a $b $c
ADDED ENTRY- CORPORATE NAME (710) (R)			$a $b $c $d
ADDED ENTRY- MEETING NAME (711 (R)			$a $c $d
ADDED ENTRY – UNIFORM TITLE (730) (R)			$a
LOCATION (852)	1	#	$a
ACCESSION NO. INCL. DT. (901)			$a 63 $b 7-10-07 $c
CALL NO. (902)			$a 005.43 N99
SUBJECT HEADIN DEFINED BY (903)			$a S.Das
ENTERED BY (904)			$a S.Das
VERIFIED BY (905)			$a S.Das

NB. #= Put blank. R means Repeatable. NR means Not Repeatable

EXAMPLE 61

THE INTERNET FOR ABSOLUTE BEGINERS

Designed, Written and Produced by

Mike Loyal

ASLIB

2001

O.I.: The Association for Information Management (ASLIB). Contain – 2 disks (double sided, double density $3^{1/2}$ in, Floppy disks). System requirement – IBM. Compatible PC with Windows 3.1, 4MBRAM, 386 or above, 7MB Hard drive space, VGA or above and a windows compatible mouse or other devices.

MARC21: BIBLIOGRAPHIC FORMAT

LEADER (M):

n	m	m	a
Record Status	**Type of record**	**Bibliographical level**	**Descriptive Catg.Form**

CONTROL FIELD –MONOGRAPH & SERIAL (008)

n			a	f
Type of Date	**Date1**	**Date2**	**Place of Publ.**	**Illustration**	**Target Audience**

#						#	
Form Of Item	**Nature of Contents**	**Govt. Pub.**	**Conf. Pub.**	**Festschrift**	**Index**	**Undefined**	**Literary Form**

	e n g	#	
Biography	**Language**	**Modified Record**	**Cata. Source**

NAME OF THE FIELD INCL. MARC21 TAG	INDICATORS 1	2	DATA WITH SUBFIELD IDENTIFIERS
ISBN NO. (020) ®	#	#	$a $c
ISSN (022) ®			$a
DEWEY DECIMAL CLASSIFICATION NUMBER (082) ®	0	#	$a 004.678 $b 20th ed
MAIN ENTRY-PERSONAL NAME (100) (NR)			$a Loyal, Mike $b $c
MAIN ENTRY –CORPORATE NAME (110) NR			$a $b $c $d $n
MAIN ENTRY – MEETING name (111) (NR)			$a $c $d $e $n
MAIN ENTRY – UNIFORM TITLE (130) (NR)			$a $d $k $l $n
KEY TITLE(222)			$a $b
TITLE STATEMENT (245) (NR)			$a The internet for absolute beginners [computer file] $c written and produced by Mike Loyal
EDITION STATEMENT (250) (nr)	#	#	$a

PUBLICATION DIST. ETC.(260) ®	3	#	$a S.I. $b ASLIB $c
PHYSICAL DESC. (300) ®	#	#	$a 2 computer disk $b double sided and double density $c 3 ½ in.+ $e 1 floppy disc
SERIES STATEMENT/ ADDED ENTRY-TITLE (440) ®	#		$a
SERIES STATEMENT (490)®			$a
GENERAL NOTE (500) ®	#	#	$a System requirements: IBM compatible PC with windows 3.1; 4MBRAM 386 or above; 7MB hard drive space; VGA or above and a windows compatible mouse or other devices
CONTENTS NOTE (505)®			$a
SUBJECT ADDED ENTRY-PERSONAL NAME (600) ®			$a $b $c
SUBJECT ADDED ENTRY-CORPORATE NAME (610) ®			$a $c $d
SUBJECT ADDED ENTRY-TOPICAL NAME (650) ®	#	0	$a Internet (computer network) $v $x $y $z

SUBJECT ADDED ENTRY- GEOGRAPHIC NAME (651) ®			$a $v
ADDED ENTRY- PERSONAL NAME (700) ®			$a $b $c
ADDED ENTRY- CORPORATE NAME (710) ®			$a $b $c $d
ADDED ENTRY- MEETING NAME (711 ®			$a $c $d
ADDED ENTRY – UNIFORM TITLE (730) ®			$a
LOCATION (852)	1	#	$a
ACCESSION NO. INCL. DT. (901)			$a 64 $b 7-10-07 $c
CALL NO. (902)			$a 004.678 P01
SUBJECT HEADIN DEFINED BY (903)			$a S.Das
ENTERED BY (904)			$a S.Das
VERIFIED BY (905)			$a S.Das

NB. #= Put blank. R means Repeatable. NR means Not Repeatable

EXAMPLE 62

OXFORD ECONOMIC ATLAS OF THE WORLD

Prepared by the

Economist Intelligence Units and the Cartographic
Department of the Clive Press

THIRD EDITION

New York

Oxford University Press

2002

O.I.: Scale varies. It is published from New York. Preliminary pages viii, textual page 26. Height- 27 cm.

MARC21: BIBLIOGRAPHIC FORMAT

LEADER (M):

n	e	m	a
Record Status	**Type of record**	**Bibliographical level**	**Descriptive Catg.Form**

CONTROL FIELD –MONOGRAPH & SERIAL (008)

n			n y u	a	f
Type of Date	**Date1**	**Date2**	**Place of Publ.**	**Illustration**	**Target Audience**

#						#	
Form Of Item	**Nature of Contents**	**Govt. Pub.**	**Conf. Pub.**	**Festschrift**	**Index**	**Undefined**	**Literary Form**

	e n g	#	
Biography	**Language**	**Modified Record**	**Cata. Source**

NAME OF THE FIELD INCL. MARC21 TAG	INDICATORS 1	2	DATA WITH SUBFIELD IDENTIFIERS
ISBN NO. (020) (R)	#	#	$a $c
ISSN (022) (R)			$a
DEWEY DECIMAL CLASSIFICATION NUMBER (082) (R)	0	#	$a 912 $b 20th ed
MAIN ENTRY-PERSONAL NAME (100) (NR)			$a $b $c
MAIN ENTRY – CORPORATE NAME (110) NR			$a $b $c $d $n
MAIN ENTRY – MEETING name (111) (NR)			$a $c $d $e $n
MAIN ENTRY - UNIFORM TITLE (130) (NR)			$a $d $k $l $n
KEY TITLE(222)			$a $b
TITLE STATEMENT (245) (NR)			$a Oxford economic atlas of the world[map] $c Prepared by the Economist Intelligence Units and the Cartographic Department of Clive Press

EDITION STATEMENT (250) (nr)	#	#	$a 3rd ed
PUBLICATION DIST. ETC.(260) ®	3	#	$a New York $b Oxford University Press $c
PHYSICAL DESC. (300) ®	#	#	$a 1 atlas (viii, 26p.) $b col. $c 27 cm $e
SERIES STATEMENT/ ADDED ENTRY-TITLE (440) (R)	#		$a
SERIES STATEMENT (490)(R)			$a
GENERAL NOTE (500) (R)	#	#	$a
CONTENTS NOTE (505)(R)			$a
SUBJECT ADDED ENTRY-PERSONAL NAME (600) (R)			$a $b $c
SUBJECT ADDED ENTRY-CORPORATE NAME (610) (R)			$a The Economist Intelligence Units, The Cartographic Department of Clive Press $c $d
SUBJECT ADDED ENTRY-TOPICAL NAME (650) (R)	#	0	$a Atlas $v $x $y $z
SUBJECT ADDED ENTRY-GEOGRAPHIC NAME (651) (R)			$a $v

ADDED ENTRY- PERSONAL NAME (700) (R)			$a $b $c
ADDED ENTRY- CORPORATE NAME (710) (R)			$a $b $c $d
ADDED ENTRY- MEETING NAME (711 (R)			$a $c $d
ADDED ENTRY – UNIFORM TITLE (730) (R)			$a
LOCATION (852)	1	#	$a
ACCESSION NO. INCL. DT. (901)			$a 65 $b 7-10-07 $c
CALL NO. (902)			$a 912 P02
SUBJECT HEADING DEFINED BY (903)			$a S.Das
ENTERED BY (904)			$a S.Das
VERIFIED BY (905)			$a S.Das

NB. #= Put blank. R means Repeatable. NR means Not Repeatable

EXAMPLE 63

PALUKANI PADMAVATI KATHALU

Govt. Oriental Manuscript Library
1925

O.I.: The work is in 52 folios containing 8 lines in a leaf and produced during 1924-1925. The palm leaf manuscript of Padmavati is available in the Government Oriental Manuscript Library. Contain Telegu stories.

MARC21: BIBLIOGRAPHIC FORMAT

LEADER (M):

Record Status	Type of record	Bibliographical level	Descriptive Catg.Form
n	c	m	a

CONTROL FIELD –MONOGRAPH & SERIAL (008)

Type of Date	Date1	Date2	Place of Publ.	Illustration	Target Audience
e	1 9 2 4	1 9 2 5			f

Form Of Item	Nature of Contents	Govt. Pub.	Conf. Pub.	Festschrift	Index	Undefined	Literary Form
#						#	

Biography	Language	Modified Record	Cata. Source
	e n g	#	

NAME OF THE FIELD INCL. MARC21 TAG	INDICATORS 1	2	DATA WITH SUBFIELD IDENTIFIERS
ISBN NO. (020) (R)	#	#	$a $c
ISSN (022) (R)			$a
DEWEY DECIMAL CLASSIFICATION NUMBER (082) (R)	0	#	$a 091 $b 20th ed
MAIN ENTRY-PERSONAL NAME (100) (NR)			$a $b $c
MAIN ENTRY –CORPORATE NAME (110) NR			$a $b $c $d $n
MAIN ENTRY – MEETING name (111) (NR)			$a $c $d $e $n
MAIN ENTRY - UNIFORM TITLE (130) (NR)			$a $d $k $l $n
KEY TITLE(222)			$a $b
TITLE STATEMENT (245) (NR)			$a Palukani Padmabati kathalu [manuscript] $c
EDITION STATEMENT (250) (nr)	#	#	$a
PUBLICATION DIST.	3	#	$a

ETC.(260) ®			$b $c 1924-1925
PHYSICAL DESC. (300) ®	#	#	$a [52] folio (8 lines) $b palm leaf $c $e
SERIES STATEMENT/ ADDED ENTRY-TITLE (440) (R)	#		$a
SERIES STATEMENT (490)(R)			$a
GENERAL NOTE (500) (R)	#	#	$a Available in the Government Oriental Manuscript Library, Chennai. – Contains Telegu stories
CONTENTS NOTE (505)(R)			$a
SUBJECT ADDED ENTRY-PERSONAL NAME (600) (R)			$a $b $c
SUBJECT ADDED ENTRY-CORPORATE NAME (610) (R)			$a $c $d
SUBJECT ADDED ENTRY-TOPICAL NAME (650) (R)	#	0	$a Manuscripts $v Stories $x Telegu $y $z
SUBJECT ADDED ENTRY-GEOGRAPHIC NAME (651) (R)			$a $v
ADDED ENTRY- PERSONAL NAME (700) (R)			$a $b $c

ADDED ENTRY- CORPORATE NAME (710) (R)			$a $b $c $d
ADDED ENTRY- MEETING NAME (711 (R)			$a $c $d
ADDED ENTRY – UNIFORM TITLE (730) (R)			$a
LOCATION (852)	1	#	$a
ACCESSION NO. INCL. DT. (901)			$a 66 $b 7-10-07 $c
CALL NO. (902)			$a 091 F25
SUBJECT HEADIND DEFINED BY (903)			$a S.Das
ENTERED BY (904)			$a S.Das
VERIFIED BY (905)			$a S.Das

NB. #= Put blank. R means Repeatable. NR means Not Repeatable

EXAMPLE 64

PC TUTOR

Learn to use the operating system PCDOS with Your Personal Computer

VERSON 2.10

London

Comprehensive Software Support, Inc.

2003

O.I.: Computer Program. 1 computer disk, $5^{1/4}$ in + Manual having coloured illustration and 4 pages. The Introseries. System requirements – IBM PC, XT or PC Jr and DOS1.1 or grater with 80 columns monitor 1 double sided disk drive.

MARC21: BIBLIOGRAPHIC FORMAT

LEADER (M):

Record Status	n
Type of record	m
Bibliographical level	m
Descriptive Catg.Form	a

CONTROL FIELD –MONOGRAPH & SERIAL (008)

Type of Date	n
Date1	
Date2	
Place of Publ.	l o #
Illustration	#
Target Audience	f
Form Of Item	#
Nature of Contents	
Govt. Pub.	
Conf. Pub.	
Festschrift	
Index	
Undefined	#
Literary Form	
Biography	
Language	e n g
Modified Record	#
Cata. Source	

NAME OF THE FIELD INCL. MARC21 TAG	INDICATORS 1	2	DATA WITH SUBFIELD IDENTIFIERS
ISBN NO. (020) (R)	#	#	$a $c
ISSN (022) (R)			$a
DEWEY DECIMAL CLASSIFICATION NUMBER (082) (R)	0	#	$a 005.432 $b 20th ed
MAIN ENTRY-PERSONAL NAME (100) (NR)			$a $b $c
MAIN ENTRY –CORPORATE NAME (110) NR			$a $b $c $d $n
MAIN ENTRY – MEETING name (111) (NR)			$a $c $d $e $n
MAIN ENTRY - UNIFORM TITLE (130) (NR)			$a $d $k $l $n
KEY TITLE(222)			$a $b
TITLE STATEMENT (245) (NR)			$a PC tutor[computer file] : learn to use the operating system PC DOS with your personal computer $c
EDITION STATEMENT	#	#	$a

(250) (nr)

PUBLICATION DIST. ETC.(260) ®	3	#	$a London $b Comprehensive Software Support, INC. $c
PHYSICAL DESC. (300) ®	#	#	$a 1 computer disc; 5 ¼ in.+ 1 manual (4p. $b col. Ill.) $c $e
SERIES STATEMENT/ ADDED ENTRY-TITLE (440) (R)	#		$a The Introseries
SERIES STATEMENT (490)(R)			$a The Introseries
GENERAL NOTE (500) (R)	#	#	$a System requirements: IBM PC; XT or PC Jr; DOS 1.1 or greater; 80 column monitor; 1 double sided disk drive
CONTENTS NOTE (505)(R)			$a
SUBJECT ADDED ENTRY-PERSONAL NAME (600) (R)			$a $b $c
SUBJECT ADDED ENTRY-CORPORATE NAME (610) (R)			$a $c $d
SUBJECT ADDED ENTRY-TOPICAL NAME (650) (R)	#	0	$a Computer operating system $v $x $y $z
SUBJECT ADDED ENTRY-			$a

GEOGRAPHIC NAME (651) (R)			$v
ADDED ENTRY- PERSONAL NAME (700) (R)			$a $b $c
ADDED ENTRY- CORPORATE NAME (710) (R)			$a $b $c $d
ADDED ENTRY- MEETING NAME (711 (R)			$a $c $d
ADDED ENTRY – UNIFORM TITLE (730) (R)			$a
LOCATION (852)	1	#	$a
ACCESSION NO. INCL. DT. (901)			$a 67 $b 7-10-07 $c
CALL NO. (902)			$a 005.4 32P03
SUBJECT HEADING EFINED BY (903)			$a S.Das
ENTERED BY (904)			$a S.Das
VERIFIED BY (905)			$a S.Das

NB. #= Put blank. R means Repeatable. NR means Not Repeatable

EXAMPLE 65

THE WESTERN UNITED STATES
Central United States
MAP

By

Rand NcNally and Co.

Chicago
American Oil Co.
1969

O.I.: Scale: 1:3,104,640. Height- 92×65 cm folded to 23×10 cm. It includes 15 insets. Verso of the title: Central Unite States

MARC21: BIBLIOGRAPHIC FORMAT

LEADER (M):

Record Status	Type of record	Bibliographical level	Descriptive Catg.Form
n	e	m	a

CONTROL FIELD –MONOGRAPH & SERIAL (008)

Type of Date	Date1	Date2	Place of Publ.	Illustration	Target Audience
t	1 9 6 9		c h u	a	f

Form Of Item	Nature of Contents	Govt. Pub.	Conf. Pub.	Festschrift	Index	Undefined	Literary Form
#						#	

Biography	Language	Modified Record	Cata. Source
	e n g	#	

NAME OF THE FIELD INCL. MARC21 TAG	INDICATORS 1	2	DATA WITH SUBFIELD IDENTIFIERS
ISBN NO. (020) ®	#	#	$a $c
ISSN (022) ®			$a
DEWEY DECIMAL CLASSIFICATION NUMBER (082) ®	0	#	$a 912.78 $b 20th ed
MAIN ENTRY-PERSONAL NAME (100) (NR)			$a $b $c
MAIN ENTRY –CORPORATE NAME (110) NR			$a Rand NcNally and co. $b $c Chicago $d $n
MAIN ENTRY – MEETING name (111) (NR)			$a $c $d $e $n
MAIN ENTRY – UNIFORM TITLE (130) (NR)			$a $d $k $l $n
KEY TITLE(222)			$a $b
TITLE STATEMENT (245) (NR)			$a The Western United States[map]: central United States $c by Rand NcNally and co.
EDITION STATEMENT (250) (nr)	#	#	$a

PUBLICATION DIST. ETC.(260) ®	3	#	$a Chicago $b American Oil Co. $c 1969
PHYSICAL DESC. (300) ®	#	#	$a 1 map $b :col. $c 92*65 cm folded to 23×10 cm $e
SCALE			Ca. 1: 3, 104, 640
SERIES STATEMENT/ ADDED ENTRY-TITLE (440) ®	#		$a
SERIES STATEMENT (490)®			$a
GENERAL NOTE (500) ®	#	#	$a Includes 15 insets
CONTENTS NOTE (505)®			$a
SUBJECT ADDED ENTRY-PERSONAL NAME (600) ®			$a $b $c
SUBJECT ADDED ENTRY-CORPORATE NAME (610) ®			$a $c $d
SUBJECT ADDED ENTRY-TOPICAL NAME (650) ®	#	0	$a $v $x $y $z
SUBJECT ADDED ENTRY-GEOGRAPHIC NAME (651) ®			$a United States $v Maps
ADDED ENTRY- PERSONAL NAME (700) ®			$a $b $c
ADDED ENTRY- CORPORATE NAME (710) ®			$a $b $c

			$d
ADDED ENTRY- MEETING NAME (711 ®			$a $c $d
ADDED ENTRY – UNIFORM TITLE (730) ®			$a
LOCATION (852)	1	#	$a
ACCESSION NO. INCL. DT. (901)			$a 68 $b 7-10-07 $c
CALL NO. (902)			$a 912.78 K69
SUBJECT HEADING DEFINED BY (903)			$a S.Das
ENTERED BY (904)			$a S.Das
VERIFIED BY (905)			$a S.Das

NB. #= Put blank. R means Repeatable. NR means Not Repeatable

EXAMPLE 66

SHAKESPEARE'S BRITAIN
Based on William Shakespeare's dramas

Edited and Published by

Melville Bell Grovenor

London

National Geographic Society

1965

O.I.: Single colour map drawn for National Geographic Magazine, May, 1964. An imaginary map drawn on the basis of Shakespeare's plays. Size of the map 60×45cm.

MARC21: BIBLIOGRAPHIC FORMAT

LEADER (M):

Record Status	Type of record	Bibliographical level	Descriptive Catg.Form
n	e	m	a

CONTROL FIELD –MONOGRAPH & SERIAL (008)

Type of Date	Date1	Date2	Place of Publ.	Illustration	Target Audience
t	1 9 6 5		l o #	a	f

Form Of Item	Nature of Contents	Govt. Pub.	Conf. Pub.	Festschrift	Index	Undefined	Literary Form
#						#	

Biography	Language	Modified Record	Cata. Source
	e n g	#	

NAME OF THE FIELD INCL. MARC21 TAG	INDICATORS 1	2	DATA WITH SUBFIELD IDENTIFIERS
ISBN NO. (020) ®	#	#	$a $c
ISSN (022) ®			$a
DEWEY DECIMAL CLASSIFICATION NUMBER (082) ®	0	#	$a 91 2.41 $b 20th ed
MAIN ENTRY-PERSONAL NAME (100) (NR)			$a $b $c
MAIN ENTRY –CORPORATE NAME (110) NR			$a $b $c $d $n
MAIN ENTRY – MEETING name (111) (NR)			$a $c $d $e $n
MAIN ENTRY – UNIFORM TITLE (130) (NR)			$a $d $k $l $n
KEY TITLE(222)	#		$a $b
TITLE STATEMENT (245) (NR)			$a Shakespeare's Britain[map]: based on William Shakespeare's drama $c edited & published by Melville Bell Grovenor

EDITION STATEMENT (250) (nr)	#	#	$a
PUBLICATION DIST. ETC.(260) ®	3	#	$a London $b National Geographic Society $c 1965
PHYSICAL DESC. (300) ®	#	#	$a 1 map $b : col. $c 60×45 cm $e
SERIES STATEMENT/ ADDED ENTRY-TITLE (440) ®	#		$a
SERIES STATEMENT (490)®			$a
GENERAL NOTE (500) ®	#	#	$a
CONTENTS NOTE (505)®			$a
SUBJECT ADDED ENTRY-PERSONAL NAME (600) ®			$a Grovenor, Melville Bell, ed. $b $c
SUBJECT ADDED ENTRY-CORPORATE NAME (610) ®			$a $c $d
SUBJECT ADDED ENTRY-TOPICAL NAME (650) ®	#	0	$a $v $x $y $z
SUBJECT ADDED ENTRY-GEOGRAPHIC NAME (651) ®			$a Britain $v Map
ADDED ENTRY- PERSONAL NAME (700) ®			$a $b $c

ADDED ENTRY- CORPORATE NAME (710) ®			$a $b $c $d
ADDED ENTRY- MEETING NAME (711 ®			$a $c $d
ADDED ENTRY – UNIFORM TITLE (730) ®			$a
LOCATION (852)	1	#	$a
ACCESSION NO. INCL. DT. (901)			$a 69 $b 7-10-07 $c
CALL NO. (902)			$a 912.41 K65
SUBJECT HEADINDG DEFINED BY (903)			$a S.Das
ENTERED BY (904)			$a S.Das
VERIFIED BY (905)			$a S.Das

NB. #= Put blank. R means Repeatable. NR means Not Repeatable

EXAMPLE 67

BHASYA IRUDAYAM

Brahmanana Venkateswara Swamigal

1949-1950

O.I.: The manuscript in leaf form contains 28 leaves with 8 lines in each leaf, size - 30×6 cm. The manuscript is available with C. Krishnamurthy Mudaliar, North Car Street, and Tanjore. The manuscript is in Tamil.

MARC21: BIBLIOGRAPHIC FORMAT

LEADER (M):

Record Status	Type of record	Bibliographical level	Descriptive Catg.Form
n	c	m	a

CONTROL FIELD –MONOGRAPH & SERIAL (008)

Type of Date	Date1	Date2	Place of Publ.	Illustration	Target Audience
e	1 9 4 9	1 9 5 0	# # #	#	f

Form Of Item	Nature of Contents	Govt. Pub.	Conf. Pub.	Festschrift	Index	Undefined	Literary Form
#						#	

Biography	Language	Modified Record	Cata. Source
	e n g	#	

NAME OF THE FIELD INCL. MARC21 TAG	INDICATORS 1	2	DATA WITH SUBFIELD IDENTIFIERS
ISBN NO. (020) (R)	#	#	$a $c
ISSN (022) (R)			$a
DEWEY DECIMAL CLASSIFICATION NUMBER (082) (R)	0	#	$a 091 $b 20th ed
MAIN ENTRY-PERSONAL NAME (100) (NR)			$a Swamigal, Brahmanana Venkateswara $b $c
MAIN ENTRY –CORPORATE NAME (110) NR			$a $b $c $d $n
MAIN ENTRY – MEETING name (111) (NR)			$a $c $d $e $n
MAIN ENTRY - UNIFORM TITLE (130) (NR)			$a $d $k $l $n
KEY TITLE(222)			$a $b
TITLE STATEMENT (245) (NR)			$a Bhasya Irudayam [manuscript] $c Brahmanana Venkateswara Swamigal

EDITION STATEMENT (250) (nr)	#	#	$a
PUBLICATION DIST. ETC.(260) ®	3	#	$a [S.I $b s.n] $c 1949-1950
PHYSICAL DESC. (300) ®	#	#	$a [28] leaves(8 lines) $b $c 30×6 cm $e
SERIES STATEMENT/ ADDED ENTRY-TITLE (440) (R)	#		$a
SERIES STATEMENT (490)(R)			$a
GENERAL NOTE (500) (R)	#	#	$a In Tamil. – Owned by C. Krishnamurthy Mudaliar, North Car Street, Tanjore
CONTENTS NOTE (505)(R)			$a
SUBJECT ADDED ENTRY-PERSONAL NAME (600) (R)			$a $b $c
SUBJECT ADDED ENTRY-CORPORATE NAME (610) (R)			$a $c $d
SUBJECT ADDED ENTRY-TOPICAL NAME (650) (R)	#	0	$a Manuscript $v $x Tamil $y $z
SUBJECT ADDED ENTRY-GEOGRAPHIC NAME (651) (R)			$a $v
ADDED ENTRY- PERSONAL NAME (700) (R)			$a $b $c

ADDED ENTRY- CORPORATE NAME (710) (R)			$a $b $c $d
ADDED ENTRY- MEETING NAME (711 (R)			$a $c $d
ADDED ENTRY – UNIFORM TITLE (730) (R)			$a
LOCATION (852)	1	#	$a
ACCESSION NO. INCL. DT. (901)			$a 70 $b 7-10-07 $c
CALL NO. (902)			$a 091 J50
SUBJECT HEADING DEFINEDD BY (903)			$a S.Das
ENTERED BY (904)			$a S.Das
VERIFIED BY (905)			$a S.Das

NB. #= Put blank. R means Repeatable. NR means Not Repeatable

EXAMPLE 68

THE GOLDEN CHAIN COUNCIL HIGHWAY MAP OF THE NORTHERN AND SOUTHERN MINES The Mother Lode MAP

Delineation and Cartography by

William Wintle

Murphy, California

Golden Chain Council of the Mother Lode Inc.

1971

O.I.: California Golden Chain. The Mother Lode Highway published by The Golden Chain Council of the Mother Lode Inc., Murphy, California, 1971. Height: 57×37cm folded to 22×10 cm. Scale: 1:700,000

MARC21: BIBLIOGRAPHIC FORMAT

LEADER (M):

Record Status	Type of record	Bibliographical level	Descriptive Catg.Form
n	e	m	a

CONTROL FIELD –MONOGRAPH & SERIAL (008)

Type of Date	Date1	Date2	Place of Publ.	Illustration	Target Audience
t	1 9 7 1		m u c	#	f

Form Of Item	Nature of Contents	Govt. Pub.	Conf. Pub.	Festschrift	Index	Undefined	Literary Form
#						#	

Biography	Language	Modified Record	Cata. Source
	e n g	#	

NAME OF THE FIELD INCL. MARC21 TAG	INDICATORS 1	2	DATA WITH SUBFIELD IDENTIFIERS
ISBN NO. (020) (R)	#	#	$a $c
ISSN (022) (R)			$a
DEWEY DECIMAL CLASSIFICATION NUMBER (082) (R)	0	#	$a 912.19 $b 20th ed
MAIN ENTRY-PERSONAL NAME (100) (NR)			$a Wintle, William $b $c
MAIN ENTRY –CORPORATE NAME (110) NR			$a $b $c $d $n
MAIN ENTRY – MEETING name (111) (NR)			$a $c $d $e $n
MAIN ENTRY - UNIFORM TITLE (130) (NR)			$a $d $k $l $n
KEY TITLE(222)			$a $b
TITLE STATEMENT (245) (NR)			$a The golden chain council map of the northern an southern mines[map]: mother load $c delineation and cartographic by William Wintle

EDITION STATEMENT (250) (nr)	#	#	$a
PUBLICATION DIST. ETC.(260) ®	3	#	$a Murphy, California $b Golden Chain Council of the mother load inc. $c 1971
PHYSICAL DESC. (300) ®	#	#	$a 1 map $b col. $c 57×37 cm folded to 22×10 cm $e
SCALE			ca. 1: 700,000
SERIES STATEMENT/ ADDED ENTRY-TITLE (440) (R)	#		$a
SERIES STATEMENT (490)(R)			$a
GENERAL NOTE (500) (R)	#	#	$a
CONTENTS NOTE (505)(R)			$a
SUBJECT ADDED ENTRY-PERSONAL NAME (600) (R)			$a $b $c
SUBJECT ADDED ENTRY-CORPORATE NAME (610) (R)			$a $c $d
SUBJECT ADDED ENTRY-TOPICAL NAME (650) (R)	#	0	$a Road maps $v $x $y $z
SUBJECT ADDED ENTRY-GEOGRAPHIC NAME (651) (R)			$a $v
ADDED ENTRY- PERSONAL NAME (700) (R)			$a $b

			$c
ADDED ENTRY- CORPORATE NAME (710) (R)			$a $b $c $d
ADDED ENTRY- MEETING NAME (711 (R)			$a $c $d
ADDED ENTRY – UNIFORM TITLE (730) (R)			$a
LOCATION (852)	1	#	$a
ACCESSION NO. INCL. DT. (901)			$a 71 $b 7-10-07 $c
CALL NO. (902)			$a 912.19 L71
SUBJECT HEADING EFINEDD BY (903)			$a S.Das
ENTERED BY (904)			$a S.Das
VERIFIED BY (905)			$a S.Das

NB. #= Put blank. R means Repeatable. NR means Not Repeatable

12

Bibliographical References

1. **Melvil Dewey.** Dewey decimal classification and relative index. - 20th ed. – New York : Forest press, 1989
2. **Library of Congress Subject Headings.** Prepared by the Cataloguing Policy and Support Office, Library Services. - 26th ed. – Washington D C: Library of Congress, Cataloguing Distribution Service, 2003.
3. **R.S. Aswal.** MARC 21: cataloguing format for 21st century. – New Delhi: Ess Ess Publication, 2004.
4. **Anil Kumar Dhiman.** Cataloguing of non-book materials. - New Delhi: Ess Ess Publication, 2004.
5. **Krishan Kumar.** An Introduction to cataloguing practice. 3rd rev. ed. 1998 (Reprint). Vikas. New Delhi. p.175-199.
6. **P.S.G. Kumar.** Knowledge organization, information processing and retrieval. ©2003. B.R. Publishing Corporation. Delhi. p.322 - 323.
7. **P.S.G. Kumar and Muhammad Riaz.** Cataloguing: theory and practice. ©1999. S. Chand & Company. New Delhi. p.291, 293.
8. **PRYTHERCH (Ray),** *Comp.* Harrod's librarians' glossary and reference book. 9th ed. ©2000. Gower. England. p.474-475, 748.

9. http://www.itsmarc.com/crs/gen 0001.htm
10. http://www.marc of quality.com
11 http://www.marctutorial.com
12. www.itsmarc.com/crs.htm
13. http://en.wikipedia.org/wiki/MARC_standards # MARC_formats
15. http://www.infotoday.com/il 2003/presentations/ Reudon/
16. http://www.uk oln.ac.uk/bib-man/factfile/cataloguing-formats/
17. **MARC21 for Everyone:** A Practical Guide By Deborah A. Fritz, Richard J. Fritz/ Published 2003/ALA Eiondits/ 240 pages/ ISBN 083890842X
18. **Cataloging with AACR2 and MARC21:** For Books, Electronic Resources By Deborah A. Fritz/ Published 2004/ ALA Editions/ 688 pages/ ISBN 0838909353
19. **Cataloging Correctly for Kids: An Introduction to the Tools** By Sheila S. Intner , Joanna F. Fountain, Jane E. Gilchrist/ Published 2005/ALA Editions/ 136 pages/ ISBN 0838935591
20. **Guide To MARC 21 for Cataloging Books and Serials** By Asoknath Mukhopadhyay/ Published 2007/Chandos Publishing, (Oxford), Limited,/ 490 pages/ ISBN 1843344076
21. **MARC 21:CONCISE FORMAT** Contributor Library Of Congress/ Published 2001/ Cataloging Distribution Service, Library of Congress/ ISBN 0844410543
22. **Maxwells.** Handbook for AACR2: Explaining and Illustrating the Anglo-By Robert L. Maxwell/ Published 2004/528 pages/ISBN 0838908756
23. **MARC 21: A Manual of MARC Practice for Libraries** By Beaumont and Associates Inc, Jane Beaumont/ Published 2001/ ISBN 096949095X

24. **Understanding MARC: Machine-Readable Cataloguing** By Betty Furrie/ Published 2000/ Cataloging Distribution Service, Library of Congress in collaboration with the Follett Software Company/ 29 pages/ ISBN 0844410330

25. **MARC CODE LIST FOR COUNTRIES** By Library of Congress Contributor Library of Congress/ Published 2003/ Cataloging Distribution Service, Library of Congress/ 46 pages/ ISBN 0844410837

26. **MARC 21 Content Designation for Scores and Sound Recordings** By Jay Weitz/ 2nd ed/ Belle Plaine, Minn. : Soldier Creek Press, 2001/ISBN 0936996773 9780936996776

27. **MARC 21 CATALOGUING FORMAT** By Rajinder Singh Aswal/ Published 2004/ Intl Specialized Book Service Inc /524 pages/ ISBN 8170003849

28. **MARC 21 Format for Bibliographic Data.**By Library of Congress Staff/ Published 2000/ Canadian Government Pub Centre/ ISBN 0660177714.

29. **Exchanging Bibliographic Data: MARC and other international formats** By Gredley, Ellen and Hopkinson, Alan/ Ottawa/Canadian Library Association/1990. /p. 209-225.

30. **"MARC21 Format for Bibliographic Data: including guidelines for content designation"**Prepared by Network Development and MARC Standards Office, Library of Congress, In cooperation with Standards and Support, National Library of Canada./ Washington/ Library of Congress, Cataloguing Distribution Service/1999.

31. http://www.loc.gov/marc/concise/

32. lib2.dss.go.th/elib/marc21/changes_concise.html

33. www.bnc.es/sprof/normalitzacio/marc21f/fcanvis.doc

34. waldkauz.bibliothek.uni-augsburg.de/kfe/rwd/96principl.html

35. www.loc.gov/marc/countries/

36. www.itsmarc.com/crs/coun0112.htm

37. tosun.ulakbim.gov.tr/~ugur/marc-doc/countries/

38. www.oclc.org/oclc/man/code/codetoc.htm

39. www.loc.gov/marc/umb/

40. onlinebooks.library.upenn.edu/webbin/book/lookupid?key=olbp17506

41. www.lac-bac.gc.ca/marc/s19-219-e.html

42. URL Corresponds to MARC21 Concise Format for Bibliographic Data — http://lcweb.loc. gov/marc/bibliographic/ecbdhome.html<.

43. **Cyril: expanding the horizons of MARC21**

    Authors: Jacobs, Jane W.; Summers, Ed; Ankersen, Elizabeth

    Source: Library Hi Tech, Volume 22, Number 1, 2004, pp. 8-17(10)

    Publisher: Emerald Group Publishing Limited

44. **Kokabi, M (1995)**, "The internationalization of MARC, part I: the emergence and divergence of MARC", *Library Review*, Vol. 44 No.4, pp.21-35

45. **Avram, H.D (1975)**, "Machine-Readable Cataloging (MARC) Program", Encyclopedia of Library and Information Science, Marcel Dekker, New York, NY, Vol. 16 pp.380-413.

46. **"Implementing MARC 21 for Holdings"** pp. 5 – 9 Copyright Year: 2003 Contributors: Diane Hillmann, PresenterRuth Haas, Presenter Rachel Hollis, Presenter Stephanie Schmitt, Presenter Pat Loghry, Recorder, The Serials Librarian, Volume: 44 Issue: 1/2, ISSN: 0361-526X.

47. "MARC21 for Everyone: A Practical Guide", **by Deborah A Fritz and Richard J. Fritz. Chicago: American Library Association, 2003. 188 p., $48.00., ISBN 0-8389-0842-**

X Serials Review, Volume 30, Issue 1, 2004, Pages 80-81

48. **"From MARC to MARC 21 and beyond: some reflections on MARC and the Arabic language" Author:** Khurshid, Zahiruddin**Source:** Library Hi Tech, Volume 20, Number 3, 2002, pp. 370-377(8)**Publisher:** Emerald Group Publishing Limited

49. **"Mapping CCF to MARC21: an experimental approach"**
Author: Rajesh Chandrakar

Source: Cataloging & Classification Quarterly, Volume 33, Issue 1 (June 2001), Pages: 33 - 49 /Year of Publication: 2001 ISSN:0163-9374 **Publisher:** Haworth Press, Inc. Binghamton, NY, USA